"OH, LET ME RETURN!"

Nature's Poets

CHINESE POETRY OF TWO MILLENNIA

For Viviane,
My granddaughter

"OH, LET ME RETURN!"

Nature's Poets

CHINESE POETRY OF TWO MILLENNIA

Translated by
Ha Poong Kim

sussex
ACADEMIC
PRESS
Brighton • Chicago • Toronto

Organization and translation of this volume copyright © Ha Poong Kim 2017.

The right of Ha Poong Kim to be identified as Editor and Translator of this work has been asserted in accordance with the Copyright, Designs and Patents Act 1988.

2 4 6 8 10 9 7 5 3 1

First published in Great Britain in 2017 by
SUSSEX ACADEMIC PRESS
PO Box 139, Eastbourne BN24 9BP

and in the United States of America by
SUSSEX ACADEMIC PRESS
Independent Publishers Group
814 N Franklin St, Chicago, IL 60610, USA

British Library Cataloguing in Publication Data
A CIP catalogue record for this book is available from the British Library.

Library of Congress Cataloging-in-Publication Data
Names: Kim, Ha Poong, 1928– editor, translator.
Title: Oh, let me return! : nature's poets: Chinese poetry of two millennia /
    [edited and translated by] Ha Poong Kim.
Description: Brighton ; Portland : Sussex Academic Press, 2017. | Includes
    bibliographical references and index.
Identifiers: LCCN 2017007151 | ISBN 9781845198886 (pbk : acid-free paper)
Subjects: LCSH: Chinese poetry—Translations into English. | Nature in
    literature. | Songs, Chinese.
Classification: LCC PL2518.8.N3 O4 2017 | DDC 895.11008/036—dc23
LC record available at https://lccn.loc.gov/2017007151

Typeset & designed by Sussex Academic Press, Brighton & Eastbourne.
Printed and bound by CPI Group (UK) Ltd, Croydon, CR0 4YY

Contents

CONTENTS

Preface

The phrase "Oh, Let Me Return!" in the title comes from the fourth-century Chinese poet, Tao Yuanming's best known poem, *gui qulai xi ci*.[1] Return to what? In his poem, Tao's meaning is clear: return to the country where his home and "field and garden" are. As the main theme of this selection of Chinese poems, however, I broaden his meaning—that is, "return to nature." In fact, the poet himself, after returning to the countryside, writes, in another poem, "Returning to Garden and Field,"[2] "At last, I have returned to nature [*zi ran*]." What does he mean by "nature"? Fundamentally, his meaning is quite simple, though it is common to relate it to the Daoist notion of nature. (This is, of course, no place to speak of Daoism.). The reader may be familiar with Chinese landscape paintings—the genre called *shan shui hua* ("mountain water painting"). Tao Yuanming's *zi ran* is precisely what is represented in such paintings. It is in this sense of nature when I speak of return to nature as the central theme of this anthology. Returning to nature means returning to life amid mountains and waters.[3]

In the poem "Returning to Garden and Field," Tao Yuanming compares his return to nature to a tethered bird's return to its old forest and also to the return of a fish from a small pond to its native mountain pool. Here one may easily see that the world from which the poet seeks to escape is the man-made one, which he calls the "net of dust." His opposition of human civilization to nature (of mountains and waters) is evident. I note here that our title "Oh, Let Me Return!" implies this fundamental opposition, which the reader will find throughout the poems in this collection.

Why does the tethered bird long to return to its old forest? And why does the pond fish dream of returning to its native pool? The reason is quite straightforward: their desire to fulfill their inherent nature as particular species of organism. We may analogously speak of a human being's desire to fulfill his or her nature as an organism. In this sense, nature may be viewed as humanity's natural habitat, where we find fulfillment of our species nature, and thus joy of life as organisms. Of course, this does not mean that the satisfaction of human nature necessarily precludes any form of communal existence or even any social conventions. In fact, some social conventions may enhance the possibility of satisfying certain inborn desires or needs. But I want to stress here the simple fact that all human societies that have ever existed have limited people's unhindered fulfillment of their basic needs and desires: hence, poems, folksongs and ballads from all cultures that express longing for release from restricting social systems. I recognize in such voices calls for return to life in nature.

The nearly three millennia of Chinese literature have left us tens of thousands of songs and poems. In many of them I recognize voices for a *return* to nature and also happy *expressions* of life in nature, as I hear in them cries of life spirit, as in the songs of birds and insects as well. Of course, we do hear expressions of human spirit in all genres of Chinese lyricism, but especially in pastoral poems (*tianyuan shi*) and nature poems (*shan shui shi*).

This book has two parts. In Part One, I translate songs from the two oldest anthologies of poetry in China: the *Shi Jing* and the *Chu Ci*. These two works are generally considered the earliest ancestors of Chinese poetry, representing its two traditions from a formal or stylistic standpoint. Perhaps, it might be difficult for my reader to recognize their differences, since the formal aspects (e.g., the number of characters in each line) are the sort of thing which can hardly be translated from Chinese into English. It may be noted that the songs in the *Shi Jing* are all anonymous, whereas nearly a half of the poems in the *Chu Ci* were written by Qu Yuan, the first known poet of China. Included in this part are also half a dozen anonymous poems from the Han period (206 BCE–220 AD).

Part Two is the main part of this book, in which I translate nearly 250 poems by thirty-three poets, beginning with Tao Yuanming of the Eastern Jin (317–420). Included here are not only the well-known poets of the Tang (618–906) and Song (960–1279) periods, such as Wang Wei, Li Bai, Du Fu, Bai Juyi, Su Shi and Lu You, but also twenty some lesser known poets, including Gao Qi of the early Ming. Tao Yuanming occupies an important place in this selection, especially as the poet of the two long poems mentioned earlier. I consider him a poet of nature in its broadest sense. In fact, all the later poets included here did pay homage to him, one way or another—that is, as a poet of nature. In this respect, Tao Yuanming was the progenitor of them all.

The reader will find the poems and songs included in this collection—some joyous, some lamenting, some indignant, some melancholy—all expressions of the same life spirit. Because I believe this spirit is present in all humans, regardless of place and time, I am confident that their voices will speak to every reader. But how successful am I in making these voices of Chinese poets audible to my English readership?

There are two points on which most translators of Chinese poetry seem to agree. First, in view of the obvious differences not only between Chinese and English, but also between their poetic conventions, these translators realize that it is unavoidable that certain elements in the original be sacrificed in translation. The question is what elements? We come to the second point. It may be obvious that most formal elements such as rhyme and meter cannot possibly be reproduced. What about the contents (or meaning) of a given poem? Most translators agree that the contents be transferable in principle from one language to another. But how? On this question, their opinions diverge. For example, some allow free or interpretive rendering, while others insist on literal translation. As far as I am concerned, I must say, I try to be as truthful as possible to the original poem, minimizing any interpretive element in the resulting translation. Is this to be "literal"?

I believe Arthur Waley is right in writing that "the soul of poetry" is imagery.[4] Clearly, to be truthful to the original must mean, above all, accurately to convey its imagery in the translation. More than anything else, this has been my concern in this work. However, the syntactical difference between the two languages raises a particular problem, namely, what Professor W-L Yip calls the "syntactically uncommitted" nature of imagery in Chinese poetry.[5] By this he means that its images are typically "juxtaposed," so that it is up to the reader himself or herself to perceive their relationship, e.g., whether they are in a relation of contrast or of similarity.[6] Though this is no place to review Yip's position in any detail, I would like to note the issue as he presents it, for I believe the issue has generally been ignored by many English translators of Chinese poetry, with unfortunate consequences. I agree with Professor Yip on this, and in my translations I have tried to retain as much as possible the "syntactically uncommitted" images, though this may have produced lines that might irritate my English-speaking readers. His main point is that English syntax does not permit, as a rule, the simple juxtaposition of images, so that most English translators tend to violate this syntactical uncommittedness by connecting two juxtaposed images by using such connectives as "though," "but" and "as." But to do this, Yip argues, is to deprive the reader of a characteristic part of the aesthetic experience of Chinese poetry, namely, of discovering oneself the relation between the images juxtaposed in it. He thus calls for "syntactical freedom" in English.

I like this idea of "syntactical freedom" in poetry, but I am not sure how it can be accomplished. True, syntax is, like all matters of language, a sort of convention, but the sort that must grow through use, i.e., tradition; it cannot be changed by fiat or even by mere agreement among some innovative few. Furthermore, translators are not creators but transmitters, and must work fundamentally within the bounds of the existing syntax for their readers. My solution regarding the issue is simple: to present juxtaposed images in Chinese poems, *as they are*, in English, as long as this does not *seriously* disturb the English reader's poetic sense, and, when this is not possible, to be ready to provide appropriate connectives, even at the risk of mistranslation. My readers will indeed see many instances of such juxtaposition in this book. Having taken this approach, I am hoping that at least some readers will begin to experience the strange joy of perceiving the poetic universe of uncommitted images. In reality as in pictures, I believe that images *simply* present themselves to us, and that it is the perceiver who *relates* them in terms of contrast or resemblance, or whatever comes into his or her head.[7]

A brief note on the frequent occurrence of onomatopoeia in Chinese poetry, especially in the adjectival or adverbial use of characters, often by doubling. In some such cases (e.g.: *xiao xiao*; *xiao se*), I have reproduced the Chinese sounds in my translation. I believe the presence of onomatopoeia is pertinent in poetry. But what may be "onomatopoeic" to the Chinese ear may not be so to the English reader. In such instances, the reader may simply ignore the occurrence. I usually convey the sense in English in the sentence where onomatopoeia occurs.

A word on the Appendix on Thoreau. Many readers may find it out of place. As far as I know, he seems to have never read any Chinese poet. But wasn't Thoreau really a poet of nature? Would he not have deeply appreciated many of the poems in this anthology?

Finally, my many thanks to the poet Elena Georgiou for editing this work.

HA POONG KIM

Notes to the Preface

1   See Appendix 1: "Oh, Let Me Return!"
2   See below.
3   One major genre of Chinese poetry is called *shan shui shi* ("mountain water poem"), which corresponds to *shan shui hua*.
4   Arthur Waley, "The Method of Translation," included in his translation: *A Hundred and Seventy Chinese Poems* (London: Constable & Co., 1918), p. 19. See also A. C. Graham, "The Translation of Chinese Poetry," included in his translation: *Poems of The Late T'ang* (New York: New York Review of Books, 1965).
5   See Wai-lim Yip, trans., *Chinese Poetry* (Berkeley: University of California Press, 1976), esp. "Translating Chinese Poetry: The Convergence of Language and Poetics—A Radical Introduction," and also his *Ezra Pound's Cathay* (Princeton: Princeton University Press, 1969), esp. Chap. 1: "The Chinese Poem: Some Aspects of the Problem of Syntax in Translation."
6   Yip cites as an example of "syntactically uncommitted" images the following well-known first line of Du Fu's poem "Spring View": *guo po shan he zai* (country/ ruined/ mountain/ river/ exist). In the original, one finds two images in juxtaposition, simply one after another, that is, "syntactically uncommitted." Ignoring this, one translator, for instance, translates it as: "*Though* a country be sundered, hills and rivers endure." (See Yip, *Chinese Poetry*, p. 23.)
7   See Appendix 2: "Images Beyond Syntax."

Note on Spelling and Pronunciation of Romanized Chinese

This book uses the Romanizing system of Chinese called *Pinyin*. Some of the rules of spelling and pronunciation are quite different from the ways in which English words are usually expected to sound in view of the spelling. The following short list of spelling may help those unfamiliar with the system come close to the original sounds of certain Chinese consonants.

c	=	*ts* as in ten*ts*
ch	=	*ch* as in *ch*irp
j	=	*j* as in *j*eep
q	=	*ch* as in *ch*eese
x	=	*sh* as in *sh*oe (very soft, nearly voiceless)
z	=	*ds* as in li*ds*
zh	=	*j* as in *j*erk

Part One

THE TRADITION

1. SONGS from the *SHI JING*

The *Shi Jing* is the oldest anthology of Chinese poetry. It contains 305 songs of ancient China (12th–7th century BCE), traditionally believed to have been compiled by Confucius. It has four parts. Of the songs selected from this work, all except the last two come from the first part, *Guo Feng*, and the last two from the second part, *Xiao Ya*. All anonymous, they are mostly folksongs of the pre-Confucian China. One distinct feature of the songs in the *Shi Jing* is that each line consists of four characters. This ancient form changes, as later songs or poems will have generally five or seven characters in each line. Another common feature of the *Shi Jing* songs is that it typically begins with reference to some natural phenomena or scenes, such as mountains, plants, birds and animals. The reader of Chinese poetry may easily recognize this feature in later poems/songs as well.

1. *GUAN GUAN*, OSPREYS

Guan guan, cry the ospreys
On the isle of the river.
Lovely is this fine maiden,
Fit match for a nobleman.

Long and short grow water mallows,
Left and right, she seeks them.
Lovely is this fine maiden,
Day and night, you long for her.

You seek her but don't get her,
Day and night you think of her.
How sad! How sad!
Turning and tossing on your side.

Long and short grow water mallows,
Left and right, she gathers them.

Lovely is this fine maiden,
Play *qin se*,[8] let us befriend her.

Long and short grow water mallows,
Left and right, she chooses them.
Lovely is this fine maiden,
Beat *zhong gu*,[9] let us delight her.

20. PLUM THROWING

I am throwing the plums,[10]
Ah, seven of them left.
Any man desiring me,
This is your fine chance.

I am throwing the plums,
Ah, three of them left.
Any man desiring me,
Now is your chance.

I am throwing the plums,
Ah, the bamboo basket is empty.
Any man desiring me,
It's time to say so.

---

[8] *Qin* and *se*, two common musical instruments, are often referred to in combination, as in this line. They look similar, but *qin* has seven strings, and *se* twenty-five.

[9] *Zhong* and *gu*, again two common musical instruments, are also often referred to together, as in this line. Separately, *zhong* means "bell," and *gu* "drum." Note that bells in the Far East are generally to be beaten, like drums, to produce sounds.

[10] According to the custom of the time, young women would throw plums or other fruits at men they liked. See No. 64, "Quince."

4

34. THE GOURD HAS BITTER LEAVES

The gourd has bitter leaves,
The ford is deep to cross.
If it's deep, take off your clothes,
If it's shallow, tuck up your skirt.

The ford is in full flood,
Wistful is the pheasant's call.
So why not let the axle get wet?
The pheasant is seeking her mate.
In unison the geese are crying,
Sunrise, it's daybreak.
Young man, if you seek your bride,
Cross the ice before it breaks away.

The boatman beckons, calling.
Others may cross, not I,
Others may cross, not I.
I will wait for my girl.

40. NORTH GATE

I go out the north gate,
Deep in my despair,
Utterly destitute, impoverished.
Nobody knows my misfortune.
All is over.
Truly, it's Heaven's doing,
Why speak of it?

The king's business comes to me,
Government business is piled on me.
I come home from work,
Everybody in the house blames me.
All is over.
Truly, it's Heaven's doing,
Why speak of it?

The king's business is sent down to me,
Government business keeps piling on me.
I come home from work,
Everybody in the house reproaches me.
All is over.
Truly, it's Heaven's doing,
Why speak of it?

45. CYPRESS BOAT

Afloat is that cypress boat
In the middle of the river.
That man, two hanging locks over his brow,
Will truly be my mate.
Till death I vow no one else will be.
Oh Mother, oh Heaven,
You don't understand my heart.

Afloat is that cypress boat
Near the river bank.
That man, two hanging locks over his brow,
Will truly be my companion for life.
Till death I vow no one else will be.
Oh Mother, oh Heaven,
You don't understand my heart.

49. HOW QUARRELSOME THE QUAILS

How quarrelsome the quails!
How rapacious the magpies!
How mean this man!
I am to call him "brother"!

How rapacious the magpies!
How quarrelsome the quails!
How mean this man!
I am to call him "lord"!

52. LOOK AT THE RAT

Look at the rat, it has a skin.
A man without etiquette,
A man without etiquette,
What is he doing without dying?

Look at the rat, it has teeth.
A man without decency,
A man without decency,
What is he waiting for without dying?

Look at the rat, it has a body.
A man without propriety,
A man without propriety,
Why doesn't he die quickly?

64. QUINCE

She threw me a quince,[11]
In return I gave her a red *ju* jade.
Not in return,
But to show my love to her forever.

She threw me a peach,
In return I gave her a fine *yao* jade.
Not in return,
But to show my love to her forever.

She threw me a plum,
In return I gave her a dark *jiu* jade.
Not in return,
But to show my love to her forever.

---

[11] See p. 4, n10.

66. HE IS GONE TO SERVICE

He is gone to service.
I don't know how long,
Oh, when will he come?
The chickens are gone to roost,
Another evening,
The sheep and cows are coming down.
He is gone to service,
How can I help thinking of him?

He is gone to service,
What day, which month,
When will I see him?
The chickens are on their perches.
Another evening,
The sheep and cows are down.
He is gone to service,
I hope he doesn't go hungry and thirsty.

76. PLEASE, ZHONGZI

Please, Zhongzi,
Don't climb over the village wall,
Don't break the willow-trees we have planted.
Not that I am concerned with them,
I am afraid of my parents.
I love you, Zhongzi,
But I am afraid
Of what my parents will say.

Please, Zhongzi,
Don't climb over our fence,
Don't break the mulberry-trees we have planted.
Not that I am concerned with them,
I am afraid of my brothers.
I love you, Zhonzi,

But I am afraid
Of what my brothers will say.

Please, Zhongzi,
Don't climb into our garden,
Don't break the spindle trees we have planted.
Not that I am concerned with them,
I am afraid of what people say.
I love you, Zhongzi,
But I am afraid
Of what people will say.

110. I CLIMB THAT WOODED HILL

I climb that wooded hill,
I look toward where my father is.
My father says, Ah, son,
You will be on duty day and night, without a break.
I pray, be careful,
Come back home, don't die.

I climb that bare hill,
I look toward where my mother is.
My mother says, Ah, son,
You will be on duty day and night, without sleep.
I pray, be careful,
Come back home, don't get killed.

I climb that hilltop,
I look toward where my brother is.
My brother says, Ah, brother,
You will be on duty day and night, but never be alone.
I pray, be careful,
Come back home, don't die.

113. BIG RAT

Big rat, big rat!
Don't eat our millet!
For three years we have labored for you,
Yet you have never looked at us.
At last we are going to leave you
For that joyful land.
Joyful land, joyful land!
Where we will have our place.

Big rat, big rat!
Don't eat our wheat!
For three years we have labored for you,
Yet you have never shown us generosity.
At last we are going to leave you
For that joyful kingdom.
Joyful kingdom, joyful kingdom!
Where we will have our due.

Big rat, big rat!
Don't eat our rice seedlings.
For three years we have labored for you,
Yet you have never recognized our hardship.
At last we are going to leave you
For that joyful country.
Joyful country, joyful country!
Where no laments are sung.

118. FIREWOOD FAST BUNDLED

The firewood fast bundled,[12]
The Three Stars[13] are up in the sky.
Tonight, what a night!
Here this fine man is with me.
Ah, ah!
What am I to do with this fine man?

The hay fast bundled,
The Three Stars are at the corner.
Tonight, what a night!
Here we enjoy our joyous union.
Ah, ah!
What am I to do with this joyous union?

The brushwood fast bundled,
The Three Stars are at the door.
Tonight, what a night!
Here this beautiful man is with me.
Ah, ah!
What am I to do with this beautiful man?

121. BUSTARDS IN THE SKY

Xiao xiao, quietly the bustards in the sky,
They come down on the oak clump.
The king's work never ceasing,
We cannot plant the millet.
Whom can our parents rely on?
Oh, the blue sky so far away!
When will we be home?

---

[12] "The firewood fast bundled" (also the similar first lines in the other stanzas of the song) stands for marriage. Accordingly, this song is commonly read as the excitement and joy at the wedding night. I have read *liang ren* in the first stanza as "good man" and *can zhe* in the last verse as "beautiful man," only because no gender-free expressions in English would sound quite natural. But the two Chinese words are used here gender-free. Therefore, the song may be sung not only by the bride but also by both the bride and bridegroom together.

[13] Orion's Belt.

Xiao xiao, quietly the bustards flying,
They come down on the thorn-bushes.
The king's work never ceasing,
We cannot plant the millet.
What will our parents eat?
Oh, the blue sky so far away!
When will all this come to an end?

Xiao xiao, quietly the bustards in the sky,
They come down on the mulberry field.
The king's work never ceasing,
We cannot plant the rice.
What can our parents relish?
Oh, the blue sky so far away!
When will we have our days in peace?

136. WANQIU

How resplendent everybody is
On the hilltop of Wanqiu!
Truly a delightful sight!
Never to forget.

Kan kan, the drum beating
At the bottom of Wanqiu.
Be it winter, be it summer,
We all dance, waving egret feathers in our hands.

Kan kan, the vat beating
On the way up Wanqiu.
Be it winter, be it summer,
We all dance, waving egret feathers in our hands.

137. ELMS OF THE EAST GATE

The elms of the East Gate,
The oaks of Wanqiu.
The daughters of the Zizhong
Are dancing under the trees.

This chosen morning so gorgeous!
The Yuan daughters of the south side,
No longer spinning hemp,
Are dancing in the market.

Let's go, this beautiful morning!
Join the crowd!
You look as lovely as the hollyhock,
You gave me a handful of pepper seeds.[14]

140. WILLOWS OF THE EAST GATE

The willows of the East Gate,
How lush their leaves!
At dusk we were to meet there,
But how bright is that morning star!

The willows of the East Gate,
How dense their leaves!
At dusk we were to meet there,
But how twinkling is that morning star!

156. EASTERN MOUNTAINS

We went to the eastern mountains,[15]
For long I didn't return home.

---

[14] As a token of love.
[15] On a military campaign.

Now I am back from the east,
It's drizzling and drizzling.
While in the east, longing to come home,
My mind was sad, thinking of the west.
Now, you have made me those clothes,
No more that bamboo piece in my mouth.[16]
A wriggling silkworm
I was in the mulberry field for so long.
All curled up I slept alone
Under that wagon.

We went to the eastern mountains,
For long I didn't return home.
Now I am back from the east,
It's drizzling and drizzling.
The fruit of that snake-gourd
Is reaching the eaves,
Wood lice crawling in the rooms,
Spider webs on the door,
The field turning into a deer ground.
Witch fire flying at night,
All nothing to fear,
Rather, I missed them.

We went to the eastern mountains,
For long I didn't return home.
Now I am back from the east,
It's drizzling and drizzling.
A stork is crying on the anthill,
Wife, sighing in the house,
Washes, sweeps, closes the cracks,
At last I am back from the campaign.
Those bitter gourds, dangling,
Have spread over chestnut firewood.
I haven't seen them
Already for three years.

---

[16] During the military campaign, a soldier was given a chopstick-like bamboo
piece to keep in his mouth. This was to prevent him from groaning.

We went to the eastern mountains,
For long I didn't return home.
Now I am back from the east,
It's drizzling and drizzling.
An oriole in flight,
Its wings shining bright.
My wife on her way to our wedding,
Her horses, brown and yellow.
Her mother had tied her girdle strings,
How splendid was the ceremony!
How blissful was our matrimony then, so new!
How is it now, old?

230. PRETTY YELLOW ORIOLES

Pretty yellow orioles
Perch on that hill slope.
Long is the road,
I am exhausted. What am I to do?
Give him drink, give him food,
Teach him, scold him.
Order the rear wagon,
Tell him to get on it.

Pretty yellow orioles
Perch on that hill corner
How dare would I shirk marching?
I fear I cannot go on.
Give him drink, give him food,
Teach him, scold him.
Order the rear wagon,
Tell him to get on it.

Pretty yellow orioles
Perch on the hillside.
How dare would I shirk marching?
I fear I cannot make it to the end.

Give him drink, give him food,
Teach him, scold him.
Order the rear wagon,
Tell him to get on it.

234. WHAT PLANT DOESN'T TURN YELLOW?

What plant doesn't turn yellow?
What day don't we march?
What man isn't taken to
This campaign in the four directions?

What plant doesn't turn black?
What man isn't to be pitied?
Alas, we soldiers alone
Are treated like nonhumans.

Neither buffaloes nor tigers,
Yet we prowl in the wilds.
Alas, for us soldiers,
Day and night, no rest.

The foxes carrying their bushy tails
Roam through the thick grass.
Pushing wooden barrows,
We march on these highways.

---

[17] The meaning of the title "*Li Sao*" has been variously interpreted. I follow
Wang Yi in my translation. David Hawkes gives the English title
"Encountering Trouble" to *Li Sao*, in his *The Songs of the South*. This is perhaps
the prevailing reading of the title.

[18] One of the legendary five *di* of ancient China. The original meaning of *di* was
god, but later, since the time of Qin Shi-huang (3rd c. BCE), *di* came to mean
"emperor." In this line, Qu Yuan is respectfully referring to his legendary
ancestor.

[19] In this and the preceding line, *yin* is one of the twelve Earthly Branches (*zhi*)
used in dating. The poet is thus using the system of *gan-zhi* ("Stem-Branch") in
writing the date of his birth.

1. SONGS from the *CHU CI*: QU YUAN

The *Chu Ci* is the second oldest anthology of Chinese poems, which represents the second tradition of Chinese poetry, after the *Shi Jing*. As we saw in the preceding section, the songs in the *Shi Jing* were all anonymous. But we know that nearly a half of the poems in the *Chu Ci*—that is, the first seven—are by Qu Yuan (340?–278? BCE), the first known poet of China. We generally equate the tradition of the *Chu Ci* itself with the style of Qu Yuan, which is also known as the *Sao* style. This name comes from the title of the first poem of the anthology, namely "*Li Sao*" ("Sorrow of Separation"). Translated below are nearly a half of this long poem, and two poems from "*Jiu Zhang*" ("Nine Pieces"), one of the seventeen chapters of the *Chu Ci*.

"*Li Sao*" is an autobiographical poem. In the first half, the poet, a scion of one of the noble families of the state of Chu during the Warring States period, laments his estrangement from King Huai, who banishes him because of a slanderous accusation against him. In the second half of "*Li Sao*," he embarks on a shamanistic journey to the spirit world in an unsuccessful quest for a mate. In real life, Qu Yuan, after banishment, spends many years of wandering in the region of Lake Dongting, and in the end drowns himself in despair in the Mi-luo River near Changsha. This biographical fact may help the reader follow my partial translation of "*Li Sao*" and also recognize the allegorical meaning underlying the second poem, "In Praise of the Orange Tree." It may also account for the persistently lamenting tone of the third poem, "Grieving at the Whirlwind."

1. SORROW OF SEPARATION[17]

Scion of Gaoyang Di,[18]
Bo Yong was my father's name,
Year of *yin*, First Month of *yin*,
On the Day of *geng yin*, I was born.[19]

My father, considering my time of arrival,
Gave me an auspicious name.
My name Zhengze,
My *zi* Lingjun,[20]

Brilliant, I already had this inner beauty,
In addition, cultivated talents.
I put on fragrant grass, *jiangli* and *bizheng*,[21]
And twined autumn orchids for my girdle.

Time so swift, as if I would never keep up with it,
I feared it would leave me behind.
In the morning, I picked magnolia on the hill,
In the evening, I gathered perennial grass on the shallows.

Sun and moon hurry on, never tarrying,
Spring and autumn, succeeding each other in turn.
Thinking of flowers withering, trees dying,
I feared my Fair One's[22] declining.

"You don't encourage the good and cast out the bad.
Why don't you change this attitude?
Ride on a spirited horse,
And let me show you the way ahead."

How pure and perfect the three kings of old!
There thrived many fragrant flowers.
They brought together mountain pepper and cinnamon,
It wasn't just weaving fragrant grass together.

---

[20] *Zi* is sometimes translated as "style" or "courtesy name," meaning the name of a person for polite use by others. Actually, according to the *Shi Ji* ("Records of the Historian"), the poet's name was Ping, and Yuan his *zi*. According to one commentator, it is customary in the *fu* poem (of which Li Sao is the prototype) to "hide one's name and take its meaning." (See Fujino Iwatomo, tr., *So Ji*, p. 26.) Zhengze means "right standard," and Lingjun "divine equity."

[21] Both unidentifiable.

[22] King Huai.

How glorious Yao and Shun!
Following the right way, they found their paths.
How licentious Jie and Zhou!
Following the shortest paths, they plunged on.

Those who banded together, how they indulged in pleasures!
Their path dark and perilous.
How would I be concerned with my own calamity?
I feared the toppling of the Lord's carriage.

Hurrying back and forth, I accompanied his carriage,
So that he would follow the footsteps of the former kings.
My fragrant Lord failed to see my deep feelings,
Instead, raged against me, believing the slander . . .

Truly I knew the danger of offering a loyal advice,
Yet I took the risk, I couldn't keep silent.
Pointing to the Ninth Heaven, I swear,
That was only for the sake of my Fair Lord.

At first, he gave me a promise,
But after, he regretted it and turned to the others.
I did not run away from our separation,
It hurt to see my Fair Lord's frequent change of heart.

—— —— —— —— ——
—— —— —— —— ——

Again and again, sobbing, in despair,
I grieve, this is not my time.
Picking tender orchids, I wipe my tears,
Tears stream, wetting my lapels.

Kneeling on my skirt outspread, I have expressed my thoughts,
I am convinced I am in the right.
A team of jade dragons, riding in a phoenix carriage,
Instantly, wind rising, I am in the air, traveling.

In the morning, I started out from Cangwu,
In the evening I arrived at the Xian Yuan,[23]
I wanted to stay a while at the gate of Heaven,
The sun was about to set.

I made Xihe[24] slow down the sun-chariot,
Yanzi[25] far ahead, so not to reach it.
My going slow, the road far to travel,
I rode up and down, looking for my ideal one.

I let my horses drink at Xian Chi,[26]
Tied the reins to the Fusang tree.
I broke a branch off the Ruo tree, chased away the sun,
For a while I roamed here and there.

I made Wangshu[27] ride ahead,
And Feilien[28] run behind me.
Yinghuang[29] announced my visit,
The thunder god told me he wasn't ready.

—— —— —— —— ——
—— —— —— —— ——

In the morning, I crossed the White River,[30]
Climbing to Langfeng[31], I was about to tie the horses.

---

[23] Meaning "Hanging Garden" in the Kunlun Mountains, believed to be a heavenly garden for gods. Note that the Kunlun Mountains meant in ancient China the westernmost part of the Middle Kingdom, and was thought of as if outside the human world, whereas Cangwu was located in today's Hunan region—that is, in the eastern part of China.
[24] The driver of the Sun-chariot.
[25] The mountain into which the sun would disappear,
[26] Pond of Heaven.
[27] The driver of the Moon-chariot.
[28] The wind god.
[29] A species of phoenix.
[30] In the Kunlun Mountians.
[31] Another heavenly garden.

Suddenly, when I turned around, my tears came down.
Sadly, no fair lady on this high hill.

Soon, I went to the Spring Palace,
Breaking a jade branch, I attached it to my girdle.
Before its flowers wither away,
I should find a maiden to attend my lady.

I made Fenglong[32] ride the clouds,
To find where Fu Fei[33] was.
I took off my girdle string to tie my words,
I made Jianxiu my go-between.

Flurries of activities, meeting and parting,
Fu Fei suddenly changed her mind, and I had no way to take her back.
In the evening she returned to Qiongshi,
In the morning, she washed her hair in the Weipan.

Guarding her beauty, how arrogant and remote!
Everyday, free of care, she was indulgent in wanton pleasures.
Though truly beautiful, no proper manners.
Come! Let's drop her and seek someone else.

———— ———— ———— ———— ————
———— ———— ———— ———— ————

Deep inside the palace, they are all beyond reach,
The wise king is also not awake.
My thoughts within, unable to express,
How can I endure this forever?

I requested Lingfen to make a divination for me
By a jade grass and bamboo twigs.
He said, "Two beautiful ones are inevitably to meet,
But who would trust your purity and follow you here?

---

[32] The cloud god.
[33] The goddess of the Lo Shui River.

"Think how vast this world is!
Would there be a lady only in Chu?
Go far abroad, and doubt not.
Who would seek a beautiful one and refuse you?

"What place would have no fragrant flowers growing?
Why should you only think of your country?"
This world is so dark, the light blinds.
Who could tell whether I am good or evil?

——— ——— ——— ——— ———
——— ——— ——— ——— ———

I wanted to follow Lingfeng's auspicious oracle,
But my mind was in doubt.
Wu Xian[34] was to descend in the evening.
Carrying fragrant pepper and refined rice for my offering,
    I went to receive him.

Hundreds of gods came down with Wu Xian,
Gods of Jiuyi Mountain also appeared to receive him.
Wu Xian, radiant, exuded a divine air,
He gave me auspicious words.

——— ——— ——— ——— ———
——— ——— ——— ——— ———

Lingfeng has already given me an auspicious oracle,
Choosing a propitious day, I shall go abroad.
Break a jade branch for my meat,
Pound jade grains for my meal.

Make my carriage with jade and ivory,
Harness winged dragons for me.
How can minds once separated be the same?
I shall go far abroad, away from this world.

---

[34] Divine shaman.

Now, my journey in the Kunlun Mountains,
The road endless, turning around and around.
The cloud-drawn banner flies in the dark shade,
The jade bridle bells ring wistfully.

In the morning I started at Tianjin,[35]
In the evening I arrived at Xiji[36].
The phoenix, reverently, carrying the pennant,
Flew high quietly *yiyi*.

Soon, I reached the desert,
Along the Red River I leisurely rode.
I beckoned the water dragons to make a bridge for me.
I asked Xi Huang[37] to let them bring me over the river.

The road was endless and full of dangers,
I made the carriages following take a small path,
I took the road to Buzhou Mountain, turning left.
We made Xihai[38] our meeting point.

Assembled here were a thousand vehicles,
Jade hub to jade hub, they galloped side by side.
My eight dragons, undulating *wan wan*,
The cloud banner hoisted, floating *wei yi*.

Suppress your wish and slow your pace,
But my spirit soars high and flies far above.
Play the Nine Songs and dance to the Shao Music,
For now, I shall make a holiday and enjoy myself.

Ascending the radiance of the heavens,
Suddenly, I looked down over my old land.
My groom sad, my horses longing,
Bending down, they kept turning back and wouldn't go.

---

[35] Ford of Heaven.
[36] The western edge of the earth.
[37] The god of the west.
[38] Meaning "West Sea," probably today's Qinghai.

Luan.[39]

Enough! There is no man in my state, no one knows me.
Why should I think of my old country?
There is none to work with for good government.
I shall follow Peng Xian[40] and go where he is.

2. IN PRAISE OF THE ORANGE TREE

God's blessed tree,
The orange tree came to this land.
By his command not to move,
It grows in the South Country, flourishing.

Deep-rooted, hard to transfer,
Its single-mindedness,
The green leaves, white blossoms,
How resplendent! It delights the beholder.

The dense branches, sharp thorns,
The round fruit, palm-full,
Green and yellow mixed,
Its pattern brilliant.

Exquisite in color, yet pure white inside,
Analogous to the man of virtue.
Luxuriant, yet without ostentation,
Beauty without impurity.

---

[39] The basic meaning of the character *luan* is "disorder." However, one finds the character also used as a term for a sort of epilogue or concluding words, in old literature of music and poetry.

[40] This line suggests Qu Yuan's decision to kill himself. According to Wang Yi's commentary, Peng Xian was a worthy of the Shang; who drowned himself when his king refused to listen to his admonition—the only historical record of his life. Qu Yuan mentions this man as his ideal man in his poem "Grieving at the Whirlwind," also translated in this section.

Oh, your youthful ideal,
So unique,
Alone standing, unchanging,
How delightful your sight!

Deep-rooted, hard to transfer,
Open-spirited, seeking nothing,
Ever reviving, alone standing,
Ever spreading, yet within bounds.

Your mind firm and judicious,
You have never erred.
Holding onto your moral power, selfless,
You have participated in Heaven's work.

As the years fade away,
I wish to stay friends with you forever.
Pure and free from debauchery,
True to our inborn grains.

Though young in years,
You are fit to be my teacher.
Your conduct, comparable to Boyi's,[41]
I hold you as my model.

3. GRIEVING AT THE WHIRLWIND[42]

I grieve at the whirlwind shaking orchid flowers,
Suffering from slanders, I am in pain.

---

[41] Boyi, a paragon of loyalty and uprightness in ancient China. After King Wu of Zhou overthrew the last king of the Shang dynasty, Boyi refused to live on grains grown under the Zhou rule and withdrew with his brother, Shuqi, into Shouyang Mountain, where the two starved to death, eating only bracken.

[42] Only the first half of this poem is translated. The part omitted includes the last section, whose authenticity has been questioned by various scholars. See Hawkes, *The Songs of the South*, pp. 179–180.

Things delicate, prone to hurt by nature,
Suffer in silence before others.

Oh, those noble thoughts of Peng Xian's[43]!
His loyalty unshakable, I will never forget it.
People change their minds ten thousand times.
   How can they hide it?
How can falsehood hold long?

Birds and beasts cry, calling to their flock,
Lush grass gives no fragrance.
Fish exhibit themselves with shiny scales,
But dragons hide their fine patterns.
Indeed, bitter and sweet herbs do not share their fields,
Orchid and sweet flag grow in seclusion,
   alone emitting their fragrance.

This good man's[44] lasting bloom!
It will shine through the ages.
How high his noble thoughts reach!
Alas, it resembles floating clouds.
How perplexing these lofty ideas!
I write this poem to illuminate them.

Only this good man in my mind,
I pluck fragrant pepper, purify my place.
Sobbing, sighing again and again,
In seclusion, I lie and meditate.

Tears streaming ceaseless,
Deep in thought, sleepless till dawn,
Long night, endless.
Though I suppress my grief, it won't go away.

---

[43] See p. 24, n40.
[44] Peng Xian's.

Rising, I take a walk quietly,
The stroll brings me some solace,
But my heart in pain, deep sigh, how piteous!
My breath choking again and again.

By twining my thoughts I make a girdle,
By weaving my sorrows, I make a chest cover,
By breaking a branch of the *ruo* tree,[45] I screen light.
I am drifting wherever the whirlwind blows.

Hazy, unable to see,
My heart is dancing like boiling water.
Holding my belt and chest cover,
I try to calm my thoughts.
Overcoming my sorrows, I wander on.

The years rush by, bringing decay,
My time, ever shrinking, approaches its end.
Fragrant grass withering, their joints falling apart,
Their fragrance lost, they are gone.

These sad thoughts may not be chastised,
That my words are not uttered for nothing will be proved.
I would rather die and vanish,
Than endlessly endure these sorrows.

The orphan cries, wiping its tears,
Abandoned, it is gone never to return.
Who could think of this without hurting?
So evident is what I have heard of Peng Xian[46]!.

---

[45] A tree believed to be growing in the west where the sun goes down.
[46] Probably of Peng Xian's ending his life by drowning. Here Qu Yuan may be foretelling darkly his own end by drowning in the Mi-luo River.

3. SONGS from "NINETEEN OLD POEMS"[47]

1. GOING ON AND ON

Going on, again going on,
We are separate though alive,
Far apart over ten thousand *li*,[48]
Living under the opposite edges of the sky.
The road hazardous and long,
Who knows when we will meet again?
The Hu horse[49] rests by the north wind,
The Yue birds[50] nests in south branches.

You left me long ago,
My dress belt becomes looser day by day.
The floating clouds hide the bright day,
The traveling one doesn't look back.
Thinking of you makes me old,
Suddenly our time is getting late.
Forsaken, I shall say no more,
Take care, feed yourself well.

---

[47] This is the title of a group of nineteen poems (*Shi Jiu Gu Shi*) brought together in *Wen Xuan* (Literary Anthology), a work compiled by Xiao Tong of Liang (502–558). These poems represent the *shi* (poetic) form of five characters (in each *line*), which gradually appears during the Han period (206 BCE–221), replacing the older four-character form as well as the irregular form of *shi*, to become one of the major poetic forms in later ages. Translated here are five poems from the group (1, 8, 13, 14, 18).

[48] One *li* is about one third of a mile.

[49] A breed of horse from the north, Xiongnu.

[50] Birds from the south, i.e., south of the Yangzi.

8. THIN AND FRAIL, A LONE BAMBOO

A lone bamboo, thin and frail,
Has taken root in the high mountain slope.
I have become your bride,
A creeper attaches itself to the club moss.
It has its time to grow,
Husband and wife the right time for their union.
Our marriage life, a thousand *li* apart,
Far, far between us, mountains and rivers.

Thinking of you makes me old,
Your canopied carriage, how slow it's coming!
How sad those orchid flowers!
Corollas inside, they flaunt their dazzling beauty.
Once their time passes, unpicked,
They will wilt away, accompanying the autumn grass.
Remain faithful,
What would I do but to be true to you?

13. DRIVING A CARRIAGE FROM THE UPPER EAST GATE

Driving a carriage from the Upper East Gate,
Far ahead I see the north cemetery outside the city-wall.
How desolate the white poplars!
Pines and cypresses on both sides of the broad road.
Buried underground are those ancient dead,
Long night in utter darkness.
In deep sleep beneath the Yellow Springs,[51]
Never to awake for a thousand years.

The seasons of Yin and Yang in perpetual transition,
Man's life, like morning dew,
Quickly ends, a brief sojourn on earth,
The human body without the firmness of metal and stone.

---

[51] Refers to the world of the dead.

For ten thousand years men have sent off each other.
Even sages and worthies cannot avoid this.
Many take nostrum to become immortals,
Find themselves victims of medicines.
Better drink fine wine
And dress yourself in white silk.

14. THOSE WHO DEPART BECOME DISTANT DAY BY DAY

Those who depart become distant day by day,
Those who arrive dearer day by day.
Step out of the city gate, look straight ahead,
You see only mounds and tombs.
Old graves are plowed for fields,
Pines and cypresses axed for firewood.
White poplars in sad wind,
Mournful sounds sink my soul.
I want to go back to my old village,
But there is no way to return.

18. A STRANGER COMES FROM FAR

A stranger comes from far,
Brings me a roll of silk.
Away from me ten thousand *li*,
His thought is still as before.
Its pattern a pair of mandarin ducks,[52]
With this roll I shall make a coverlet for us both.
Fill it with the thought of long-lasting love,
Sew it into our inseparable union,
Dip it in lacquer with gum.
Who would be able to separate this?

---

[52] Symbolizing conjugal happiness.

* * *

DRAFTED INTO THE ARMY AT FIFTEEN[53]

Drafted into the army at fifteen,
At eighty I come home for the first time.
On the road I meet a village man.
Is anyone of my family still alive?
Look far ahead, you see your home,
Pines and cypresses, mounds one after another.
A rabbit goes in the house through the dog opening in the wall,
A pheasant flies up from the ridge-pole.
In the middle of the yard is wild millet growing,
Around the well wild mallows.
I pound millet with a pestle to prepare a meal,
Pick mallows to make a soup.
The meal and soup are all ready,
I don't know whom to serve.
Going outside the gate, I look east,
Tears stream down, wetting my clothes.

---

[53] This poem, by an unknown Han poet, is not one of the "Nineteen Old Poems"
in *Wen Xuan*. It is included here along with this group; it is also a five-character
poem of the same period.

Part Two

"Oh, Let me Return!"

1. TAO YUANMING (365–427)

TIME MOVES ON, with a prefatory note

Time moves on. I stroll in late spring. The spring clothes are ready to wear.[54] All sights peaceful. My shadow in company, I stroll alone, alternately feeling joy and melancholy.

Mai mai, steadily time moves on,
Mu mu, it's a fine morning.
Putting on my spring clothes,
I stroll to the east field.
The mountains fresh from mist,
The sky somber in haze.
The wind from the south
Quickens those new shoots.

Yang yang, the water calm and full at the river crossing,
I rinse the mouth and wash.
Miao miao, far away, the distant view,
How delightful to watch.

---

[54] This sentence appears in an unusual conversation between Confucius and his pupils in the *Analects* (11:25). For the full appreciation of the poem, I cite here the relevant part of the conversation, the longest chapter of the *Analects*. The Master invites each of the four pupils in attendance to speak his mind. After three of them have spoken, the last one, Ceng Xi, says: "In late spring, when the spring clothes are all ready to wear, in company of five or six young men and six or seven boys, I would like to bathe in the River Yi, enjoy the breeze on the Rain Dance Hill, and return home singing." After hearing this, the Master sighs and says, "I am with Dian [Ceng Xi]."

People say,
If agreeable to your heart, that's good enough.
Emptying this cup,
Blissfully I enjoy myself.

Turning my eyes to the midstream,
I think of the clear River Yi.[55]
Those youths, studying together,
Return from an outing, singing carefree.
I love their peaceful spirits,
Day and night, they encourage one another.
I only deplore theirs was another world,
So distant, beyond reach.

Morning or evening,
Peace in this hut.
Chrysanthemums in rows,
The bamboo bush dense,
The lute on couch,
The unstrained wine half full in the jar.
The ages of Huang and Tang[56] are not to recover.
Sadness is only in me.

RETURNING BIRD

Hovering in the sky, the bird is returning.
He leaves his forest at dawn,
Flying far to the edge of the sky,
Resting near at cloud-covered peaks.
Fair wind not everywhere,
Turning around, he seeks the place of his heart.

---

[55] The river mentioned by Ceng Xi in the episode cited from the *Analects* in the preceding note. "Those youths" in the next line are also the youths mentioned in the episode.
[56] The legendary times of Huang Di and Yao Di.

Seeing his kin, he calls to them,
Hides in the cool shades.

Hovering in the sky, the bird is returning,
Flying this way and that way.
Though he no longer thinks of traveling far,
The sight of forests stirs his desire.
Meeting clouds, he sails up and down,
Calling, he returns.
Flying far in the sky, how blissful!
He never forgets his heart's love.

Hovering in the sky, the bird is returning,
Roaming over his familiar forest.
Why would he think of a celestial journey?
So happy to arrive at his old nest!
Though his old cronies are gone,
The calling sound of his flock pleases his ears.
At dusk the air clean
Calms his spirit.

Hovering in the sky, the bird is returning.
Perching on a cold branch, he folds his wings,
No more traveling to the distant woodland,
He roosts on a bough in the forest.
Fresh morning breeze in the air,
Birds exchange their joyous calls.
Why shoot at them with stringed arrows?
He has had enough, why would he struggle?

TRANQUILITY ON THE NINTH DAY, with a prefatory note

Living quietly, I love the name of *chong jiu* ("double ninth").
Autumn chrysanthemums fill my garden. Yet I have no means of
obtaining wine. Unwittingly I eat the flowers of double ninth.[57]
(note overleaf) I put down my thoughts in words.

Life is brief, desires are always many,
So humans delight in long life.
This day and month arrives by the progression of time,
Common folks all like the name of double ninth.
The dew cool, warm wind has ceased,
The air clear, the sky bright.
Gone are swallows, their shadows no more,
Geese arriving, the echoes of their honking in the air.

Wine can wash away a hundred worries,
Chrysanthemums alleviate the aging.
Why is the man of this hut
Just staring at his time's declining?
A wine cup collecting dust is a disgrace to the empty wine barrel,
Cold flowers[58] bloom for nothing.

Straightening my lapel, alone I chant a verse quietly,
In me well up deep feelings steadily.
Surely life of tranquility brings numerous joys,
I will stay where I am, would it amount to nothing?

RETURNING TO GARDEN AND FIELD, five poems

(1)
When young, I was out of tune with the world's way,
By nature I love hills and mountains.
By mistake I fell in the net of dust,
Thirteen years passed in a flash.
Tethered birds long for their born forest,
Fish in a pond dream of their native pool.

---

[57] The expression "double ninth" refers to the ninth day of the ninth month, and "flowers of double ninth" to chrysanthemum flowers. On this day, people would float chrysanthemum flowers on wine and drink it together with flowers. The character for number nine, *jiu*, sounds the same as the character for "long time"; hence, the number's association with "long life."
[58] I.e., chrysanthemums.

I have opened the wasteland at the edge of the south field,
My born nature still intact, I have returned to my garden and field.

The ground barely over ten *mu*,[59]
The thatched cottage eight or nine *jian*,[60]
Elms and willows shading the rear eaves,
Peach and plum trees in line before the hall.
The distant village in haze,
Faint smoke slowly rising in the desolate hamlet.
A dog barks in a back alley,
A cock crows at the tip of a mulberry tree.
My yard free of bustling,
Leisure and stillness in my empty room.
For long I lived inside a birdcage,
At last, I have returned to nature.

(2)
Out in the country rare are human contacts,
In this narrow alley few carriages come.
During broad daylight the brushwood gate shut,
In my empty room no more worldly thoughts.
At times, walking through grass on a village road
I come across someone going by.
Our eyes meet, but no idle talks,
We merely speak of mulberry leaves and hemp growing.
Day by day mulberry leaves and hemp already growing,
My field already expanding.
My constant worry frost and hail,
It may turn into a bramble field.

---

[59] Approximately 500 square meters.
[60] Usually translated as "room." But *jian* could also mean a unit of room space, approximately 2 square meters. A "thatched cottage of eight or nine rooms" would give an absurd image of a thatched mansion.

(3)

I planted beans at the foot of the South Mountain,
Grass is rampant, bean sprouts sparse.
With sunrise I rise to pull weeds,
Moonlight on my back, I return home carrying the hoe.
The path narrow and vegetation tall,
Evening dew soaks my clothes.
I don't mind soaking clothes,
I only pray my wish be fulfilled!

(4)

For long I neglected to rove mountains and waters,
Now with abandon I roam in forests and fields.
Fancifully, taking my child and nephew in tow
I walk through brushes in the abandoned fields.
Wandering on the cemetery hill,
I notice the traces of an old dwelling unmistakable.
Evidence of well and kitchen on the ground,
The remains of stumps of mulberry trees and bamboo bushes.
I ask a woodchopper,
What happened to the occupants?
The woodchopper tells me,
All dead, none surviving.
A single generation changes palaces and cities,
This is truly not an empty saying.
Human existence like a phantom,
In the end returning to nothing.

(5)

Despondent, alone, I turn around carrying my cane,
Walk down the shrubby path on the rugged hill.
The mountain creek, limpid and shallow,
Tempts me to wash my feet in.
I strain my newly brewed wine,
Kill a chicken, invite a neighbor.
Sundown, darkness fills the room,
Burning wood for our candle light.
Cheerfulness arrives, regrettably the night too short,
Already daybreak is coming.

ON A MORNING OF FIFTH MONTH, rhyming with Dai Zhubu[61]

The empty boat, oarless, drifts on and on,
The seasons' rotation endless.
The year began as if yesterday,
Yet its midpoint fast approaching.
Summer colors break forth on all things,
The north wood flourishing.
Shenping[62] has poured down the seasonal rain,
South breeze freshens the morning scene.

Having arrived, who wouldn't leave?
Life's truth is that it has an end.
Live simply till your time expires,
Would the bent elbow[63] injure your tranquility?
Life's course may be even or steep,
But follow your nature, never mind rise or fall.
Be at one with the present, it's as though you are already high up.
Why must you climb Hua Shan or Song Shan[64]?

DRINKING ALONE DURING A RAINY SPELL

The living inevitably comes to expire,
So goes the saying from time immemorial.
People say there were immortals like Chisong and Ziqiao,[65]
Where are they today?
One elder sends me wine, saying

---

[61] *Zhubu* is an office title, referring to registrar in a local administration. Dai Zhubu is an unknown person.

[62] The god of rain.

[63] Cf. *Analects*: "The Master said: Eat coarse food, drink water, and use your bent elbow for pillow. You will find happiness in it." (7:15)

[64] Both two well-known mountains, where Buddhist temples were located. *Shan* in both names means "mountain." Hereafter, as in this line, the character will not be translated when used in a mountain name.

[65] I.e., Chisong Zi and Wang Ziqiao.

Drink it and you will become an immortal.
I try it, instantly a hundred worries are gone,
A cup after another, at once I forget Heaven.
Would indeed Heaven surpass this?
Follow your true nature, nothing before it.
A heavenly crane, spreading its wondrous wings,
Travel over all eight directions instantly.
I have carried this nature since birth,
Yet I toiled forty years.
My body has long changed,
My mind still intact, what more would I say?

MOVING HOUSE, two poems

(1)
Once I desired to live in the South Village,
Not for a geomantic reason.
I had heard of many simple-spirited souls living there,
With whom I could frequently enjoy mornings and evenings.
Many years have passed since,
Today I have made the move.
A humble cottage, why must it be huge?
Sufficient, so long as it covers bed and mat.
Frequently neighbors come by,
With passion, we discuss the old days.
Together we read and enjoy fantastic passages,
Dissect and examine questionable meanings.

(2)
Spring and autumn, many fine days,
I climb hills, recite new poems.
Passing a neighbor's gate, we call to each other,
If he happens to have wine on hand, we drink together.
After the field work, we all go home,
While resting, we think of each other.
Thinking of each other we put on our robes,
Talk and laugh, no moment of boredom.

Nothing can surpass this truth.
Don't leave this place lightly.
Food and clothes one ought to provide oneself.
Strenuous tilling never cheats me.

REPLY TO LIU CHAI SANG[66]

This lean life, human contact rare,
At times, oblivious of the four seasons in transition.
The yard is full of fallen leaves,
Sadly, I realize it's already autumn.
The new sunflowers shade the north window,
The glad rice crop getting ripe in the south field.
Unless I enjoy all this now,
Who knows of the next year?
On a fine day, I tell my wife,
We shall go hiking, taking our children.

RHYMING WITH GUO ZHUBU,[67] two poems

(1)
How lush the trees in front of the hall!
They store cool shades in the middle of summer.
South wind arrives timely,
A light whirlwind blows my lapel open.
Giving up all human intercourse, I engage in leisurely activities,
Day and night, I enjoy books and the lute.
Vegetables in the garden are growing bigger and bigger,
Last year's grains are still in store.
Self-preservation should have a limit,
Going beyond sufficiency is not to be sought after.

---

[66] Liu Cheng Zhi. Chai Sang is the name of a prefecture, of which Liu is magistrate.
[67] Guo Zhubu is an unknown person. For *Zhubu*, see p. 41, n61.

Pound glutinous millet in the mortar and brew fine wine,
When the wine is brewed, I scoop it by myself.
My child at play by my side,
He picks up words but barely speaks.
This life is truly blissful,
It makes one forget the lure of flowery hairpins,[68]
Far, far above I gaze at white clouds,
How keenly I think of the ancients![69]

THE HOUSE BURNS IN SIXTH MONTH

My hut stood at the end of a back alley,
Happily it kept away glittering canopied carriages.
In the middle of summer a windstorm suddenly came,
This cottage, in the midst of trees, instantly burned down.
The whole house now gone, its roof and all,
For a shelter we keep a boat before the gate.

A clear early autumn evening,
High up the moon nearly full.
Fruit trees and vegetables have begun to grow again,
Frightened birds yet to return.
At night I linger under the moonlight, my thoughts soaring high,
In a moment I travel the ninth heaven.

I have held onto my peculiar nature since my youth,
Already for more than forty years.

---

[68] Refers to high officials of government.
[69] The last two lines refers to the *Zhuang Zi* (Ch. 12): "When the world is without Dao, the sage nurtures his De (spiritual power), and engages in leisure. After a thousand years, when he becomes weary of the world, he will leave it and ascend to the upper realm. Riding on white clouds, he will reach the village of immortals."

44

My body has decayed through transformation,
Alone my soul has long stayed quiet,
Firm from its inborn nature,
Neither a jade nor a stone as hard.

I think back to the time of Donghu.[70]
Grains left uncollected in the fields,
Bellies full, minds empty,[71]
People up in the morning, back home at dusk for sleep.
This time is long past, not to come,
For now, I am watering my garden.

ON NINTH DAY OF NINTH MONTH

Autumn slowly in decline,
How bleak! Wind and dew come in turn!
Rampant grass has stopped growing,
Trees in the yard losing their leaves.

Clear weather cleanses the air of its putrid residues,
The sky high, limitless.
Cicadas never stop their sad notes,
Geese, flying in formation, honk from high above.

Ten thousand transformations in perpetual succession,
Human life, how can it be without toil?
From time immemorial all have ended,
This thought torments my heart.

---

[70] A mythological time of plenitude and simple life.
[71] Cf. *Dao De Jing* (Ch. 3): "If you do not exalt the worthy, / You will keep the people from contention. / If you do not treasure rare goods, / You will keep them from stealing./ If you do not exhibit things that may arouse their desire, / You will keep their minds in peace./ Therefore the sage, in governing the people, / Makes their minds empty, / Their bellies full. . . ."

How am I to soothe this feeling?
Unstrained wine cheers me up for a while.
A thousand years are nothing to care about,
For now I would make this moment long-lasting.

EARLY-RICE HARVEST AT THE WEST FIELD IN NINTH MONTH

All human existence comes to one truth,
Food and clothing are surely its beginning.
Who would seek happiness
Without securing them?

Early spring, I began this yearly work right,
Probably this year will see a good crop.
Starting the day at sunrise, I work hard, though slow,
After sundown, I return home with the hoe on my shoulder.

In this mountain, severe frost and dew,
Also cold wind comes early.
Farm life, how can it be easy?
One must not escape this hardship.

My four limbs are truly exhausted,
I pray, no sudden mishap befalls me.
After washing my hands and feet, I rest under the eaves,
A bowl of wine disperses all fatigue from mind and body.

Changju and Jieni,[72] of ancient time,
Their minds and mine a thousand years apart, yet so close.
I only hope I remain like this for a long time.
Farming for oneself is not something to lament.

---

[72] A pair of recluses, who appear in *Analects* (Ch. 18).

DRINKING WINE, twenty poems

My daily life is quiet with little merriment. On top of it, evenings have
recently become rather long. By chance I have had a wine of superior
quality at home. No evenings go by without my drinking. In the
company of my shadow, I drink alone. In no time I get intoxicated. In
my merry state, I compose a few lines to amuse myself. In time, the
written sheets have accumulated to some quantity. No theme or order.
For fun I have asked my friend to rewrite them for me.

(4)
Anxiously, a bird, separated from its flock,
Still flies alone at dusk.
Nowhere to rest, roving,
Night after night, its crying so pitiful.
That heart-rending tone, longing for morning light,
Coming and going, again and again, so restless.

Spotting a lone pine tree,
It folds its wings and descends from high above.
In strong winds all trees have lost their leaves,
Only this one keeps its shade.
Having found a place to repose its body,
For a thousand years the bird will never leave this tree

(5)
This hut stands within the human habitat,
Yet no noise of carriages and horses.
How is that possible? some may ask.
The mind remote from the world, naturally, so is the place.
Plucking chrysanthemums under the east hedge,
I catch sight of the south mountain in all its serenity.
The mountain mood is best at dusk,
Birds return one after another.
In all this, one finds the true meaning of life,
I try to express it but forget the words.

(7)

Autumn chrysanthemums in fine colors,
I pick the flowers, drenching myself in dew.
Float them on the worry-forgetting thing,
Gone is my self, I have left all worldly concerns.
My cup alone at work,
When it becomes empty, the bottle tilts by itself.
After sundown, all movements come to rest,
Returned birds calling in the woods.
Carefree, I sing under the east eaves,
For now, I have regained this life.

IN OLD STYLE, nine poems

(3)

Early spring,[73] a seasonal rain,
The first thunder starts from the eastern sky.
All underground creatures frightened out of hibernation,
Plants stretching up and sideways.
Flying around in the air are swallows newly arrived,
A pair flies in my hut.
The old nest still there.
They have returned to their former residence.
Since our separation
The yard has grown wild day by day.
My mind of course not a stone.
What are your feelings?

---

[73] *Zhongchun,* the second month of the year in the Lunar Calendar, literally means "mid-spring, but is closer to "early spring" in the Western conception of spring-time.

[74] An ancient book of geography, which contains Chinese legends and mythology.

READING THE *SHANHAI JING*,[74] thirteen poems

(1)
Early summer, the plants grow tall,
All around my cottage, tree leaves dense.
Flocks of birds are delighted to come to rest,
I too enjoy my thatch-roofed hut.
The tilling already done, the planting already finished,
Time has returned for me to read my books.
My narrow lane allowing no deep ruts,
My visitors turn around their carriages.
Welcoming them, I pour out spring wine,
Serve them greens from my own garden.
Gentle rain from the east,
Pleasant breeze accompanying.
We go over the Story of the Zhou King,[75]
Glance over the pictures of the *Shanhai Jing*.
In no time we travel around the entire universe,
If this doesn't give one pleasure, what would?

OH, LET ME RETURN!,[76] with a prefatory note

My house was poor. Farming was not sufficient to support us. The house was full of children, but the grain storage was empty. As for my resourcefulness, I had acquired no talent for that. My relatives and friends urged me to seek employment at the government office. With much resoluteness, I decided to do so, but had no way to find it.

That was a time of political upheaval, so that all the principalities were in search of men of talent. Thanks to my uncle, who was concerned with my poverty, I finally got a job at a small county office. The time was still in turmoil. And I was not inclined to work too far away from

---

[75] A story of King Mu of Zhou, which narrates his adventurous travel around his kingdom.
[76] See Appendix 1: "Oh, Let Me Return!" for my translation of the original title *"gui qulai xi ci."*

home. Pengze was about thirty miles away. The work gave me the benefit of use of public land, where I could produce enough grain to brew my own wine. So I took it.

But within a few days on the job, I already missed home and was already thinking of returning. Why? My inborn nature [*xing*] is to follow the way of nature (*zi ran*), and not to exert myself for anything willfully. Even were I to starve and freeze, I would rather suffer hardship than going against my nature. In the past, I had also worked in public office, all for the good of [the family's many] mouths and stomachs. I resented this and felt deeply ashamed in the light of my true commitment of life. I was only hoping to find an evening when I could pack up for a trip home and run.

Some time later, my married sister suddenly died in Wuchang. Eager to go to the funeral immediately, I resigned from my post and left. From mid-August till the winter, I worked in that office for some eighty days. Thanks to this happening, I could fulfill my heart's desire. I call this piece "Oh, Let Me Return!"

Oh, let me return!
Field and garden are about to turn into wilderness, why not return?
For long I have made my spirit the slave of my body,
Why just despondent, grieving alone?
Realize not to reprove the past,
Know to pursue the future.[77]
In truth, I haven't gone far off the road,
I know I am now right, was wrong in the past.
Slowly, my boat moves on, pitching lightly,
The wind whistles by, fluttering my robe.
I ask a fellow passenger, how far to go?
To my grief, the morning light is still dim.

Seeing ahead the roof of my cottage,
Overjoyed, I run.

---

[77] Cf. *Analects*: "Jie Yu, the madman of Chu, went past Confucius, singing – Oh phoenix, phoenix/ How declined is your De/ As to the past, do not reprove it, / As to the future, you may pursue it. . . ." (18:5).

My servant welcomes me,
My boy waiting at the gate.
The footpaths have turned wild,
The trees and chrysanthemum bushes still standing.
Carrying my child, I enter the house,
Wine fills the barrel.
I bring jug and cup to drink,
Looking at the tree branches in the yard, I smile.
Leaning to the south window, self-contented,
I relish the coziness of this small space.
My garden increases its charm day by day,
The gate, though standing, always closed.
I stroll with a walking stick, stopping here and there,
From time to time, raise my head to enjoy a distant view.
Clouds idly rise from the mountain peaks,
Birds, tired of flying, know to return home.
The sun going down, dusk sets in,
Caressing a lone pine tree standing, I linger on.

Oh, let me return!
Let me end all human intercourse, no more wandering.
With the world I am out of tune,
Riding an official carriage, what would I seek?
How delightful the life stories of my relatives,
How enjoyable the lute and books, which free me from all worries!
A farmer tells me of spring's arrival,
Soon there will be work to be done in the west field.
Get the covered wagon ready,
Paddle the lone boat.
I shall enter the deep valley,
Cross the steep hill.
The trees are happy to bloom,
Springs begin to flow, murmuring.
It's the time when the ten thousand things rejoice,
I feel my life seeking to rest.

Ah, quit it all!
Your body, lodged under heaven, how much time have you still?

Why not let your mind direct your going and staying?
Why restless? Where do I want to go?
Riches and high office are not what I seek,
The celestial sphere is not to be sought after.
I envision myself strolling alone on a fine day,
Or planting my stick by my side to pull out grass.
I shall climb the east hill and whistle a long tune,
Stand by a clear stream, and recite a poem.
For a little while, I will ride on the transformation, till my time ends,
Enjoy my heaven-appointed life, why would I doubt this?

2. XIE LINGYUN (385–433)

DEPARTING FROM SHIGUANTING PAVILION AT NIGHT

I have crossed the mountains more than a thousand *li*,
Floated on the rivers nearly ten evenings.
Birds have returned, the oars at rest,
Scarce the stars, weary is the official journey.
Ting ting the foredawn moon bright,
Ling ling the morning dew dripping cold.

STOPPING AT THE SHINING ESTATE

When young, I had noble ideals,
The pursuing of things has changed me altogether.
It seems as though I had deviated from my wish yesterday,
Now twenty-four years have passed.
Lost are the purity and broadness through smudging and rubbing,
Tired, I am ashamed before the upright ones.
My ineptness and illness have combined,
Rather, to let me regain the way to peace.

I have been appointed a district magistrate by the sea,
Sailing off the course, I stop at my ancestral mountain.
I climb the hills, up and down till exhausted,
Cross the stream, repeatedly back and forth.
Soaring rocks, peak behind peak,
The shallows meandering, the beach stretching uninterrupted.
White clouds embrace the mysterious cliffs,
Alluringly, the green bamboos sway to clear ripples.

I shall build a house looking down over the river bend,
A lookout pavilion on top of the hill.
Waving my hand, I tell villagers,
In three years, I shall definitely return.

In the meantime, please plant elms and paulownias for me,
Let me realize my wish.

3. BAO ZHAO (412?-466)

HISTORICAL POEM[78]

The five great cities boast wealth and energy,
Loyang[79] nurtures fame and profit.
Millionaires never meet public execution,
Doctors of the Confucian Classics occupy high offices.

Along the twelve avenues of the capital
The tile roofs soar in rows, shining like fish scales.
Bureaucrats fly their bright cap-ribbons,
Tourists hold their reins lightly.
The morning star yet to fade away,
The covered wagons[80] are already arriving, like clouds.
What a racket the reinsmen create!
The saddled horses brighten the ground.

Cold and hot are passing phenomena,
Blooming flowers hardly more than spring's charm.
Alone Yen Junping[81] in solitude,
He and the world have abandoned each other.

IN OLD STYLE

Gather firewood in the dark bamboo grove,
Cut the sparse millet in the cold gully.

---

[78] The title merely refers to the genre of the poem, *yongshi*.
[79] The capital.
[80] Of high officials.
[81] A man of the Han dynasty, who is said to have earned his living by divination. According to legend, he quit fortune-telling each day after earning a hundred coins just enough to get by and returned home to teach the *Dao De Jing*. Here the poet may be referring to himself.

The north wind hurts my skin,
Birds, crying, arouse my melancholy thoughts.

End of the year, the land tax paid off,
Now come the other taxes one after another.
The land tax goes to Hanguguan,[82]
Straws for horses to the Emperor's hunting grounds.
The Yellow River and the Wei River, still frozen, closed to ships,
Hanguguan and Long Shan are deep in snow.
Whipping punishments from high officials,
Abusive reprimands from lowly functionaries.[83]

Don't say, I had an ambition for a canopied wagon,
And kept my head down in a horse feeder[84] till today.

---

[82] Namely, to the capital.
[83] Due to late tax payment?
[84] A metaphor for a man of talent in poverty, failing to reach high position in government.

4. WANG JI [85]

ENTERING RUO XI CREEK

Our boat moving quietly,
Sky and water spread far ahead.
Dark mist rising over the distant peaks,
The sunlight chases the counter current.
The noise of cicadas intensifies the still of the forests,
The crying of birds deepens the mystery of the mountains.
This place stirs my desire to return to nature,
The long years of my tiresome wanderings sadden me.

---

[85] Dates unknown. According to one record, Wang Ji served the ruler of Liang (502–519).

5. TAO HONGJING (452–536)

REPLY TO THE EMPEROR'S QUESTION, WHAT'S IN THE MOUNTAINS?[86]

What's in the mountains?
Over the mountains many white clouds.
They only delight me,
Wouldn't bear being brought to Your Majesty.

---

[86] A question posed to the poet by Wu Ti of Liang.

6. WANG JI (585–644)

COUNTRY VIEW

From the East Hill, a view at dusk,
I roam, wondering what I should live by.
Trees, trees, all in autumn colors,
Hills, hills, all in bright evening sun.
The shepherds are going home, driving their calves,
The hunters on horseback, their catches dangling.
Have I seen them before? None.
Singing a long tune, I think of picking bracken.

7. DU SHENYAN (645?–706)

EARLY SPRING VIEW[87]

Alone, working abroad as an official,
I am surprised to see the season's change all around.
The mist rises over the morning sea,
It's springtime. The plum trees and willows have crossed the Yangzi.
Mild air. The yellow birds[88] are singing,
Clear sunlight playing with the green rushes.
Suddenly, I hear an old tune,
Homesick, tears in my eyes.

---

[87] The full title of this poem reads: "Rhyming with Jinling Official Lu's Early Spring Scene."
[88] Orioles.

8. CHEN ZIANG (661–702)

STOPOVER AT LEXIANG XIAN

My home village is far away, beyond the horizon,
Sundown, I am alone on the road.
The open plain along the river, lost in this ancient land,
The road leads to the desolate town.
The garrison in ruin, no smoke rising.
Deep in the mountain, old trees lying.
What am I to do at this hour of gloom?
The night monkeys are crying.

9. MENG HAORAN (689–740)

STAYING OVERNIGHT BY THE JIANDE RIVER

After moving the boat, I stay overnight on the misty shore,
Sundown, the traveler's melancholy anew.
The limitless plain, the sky low over the trees,
The river clear, the moon comes nearer.

AT SPRING DAYBREAK

Sleeping in spring, unaware of daybreak,
From all around come the sounds of birds chirping.
Last night, the noise of a storm,
I wonder how many flowers fell.

ON THE WALL OF YIGONG'S *CHAN*[89] HUT

Yigong, practicing *chan*-stillness,
Put up a hut in a secluded forest.
Outside the gate a peak soaring,
Beyond the steps countless ravines.
The evening sun after a rainfall,
The green canopy in the air casts its shadow on the yard.
You see the lotus flowers so pure,
Now you know the undefiled mind.

---

[89] I.e., *zen* in Japanese. In fact, *zen* is the Japanese pronunciation of the character *chan* in Chinese.

10. QI WUQIAN (692–749)

OVERNIGHT AT LONGXING TEMPLE

Longxing Temple, night, I forgot to leave.
The pine tree, clear green by the old hall entrance.
The light bright, the abbot's room,
The beads hanging, the monks' robes.
White daylight, dharma transmission wordless,
Blue lotuses, dharma truth mysterious.
Heavenly flowers[90] falling ceaseless,
Here and there the birds flying, petals in their beaks.

---

[90] According to Buddhist legend, "heavenly flowers" are sent down after dharma talks are given by great masters.

11. ZU YONG (699–746)

AT SU SHI'S COTTAGE

This cottage in a hushed place,
Arriving, I feel the desire to retire to the mountains.
Zhongnan Shan facing the door and windows,
The Feng River reflecting the garden and woods.
The house is still under the last winter's snow,
The yard dark, though not yet dusk.
Liao liao, all in peace, outside the human world,
Sitting quiet, I listen to the spring birds.

12. SUN DI (696?-761)

STAY AT YUNMEN TEMPLE

The temple at the foot of Yunmen Shan,
Flowers deep in mist, out of this phenomenal realm.
Hanging lanterns lighted, the evening sky over a thousand peaks,
Screens rolled up, autumn over the Five Lakes.
On the painted wall, the geese are still flying,
The North Star and the Herdsman lodging in the silk window.
Perhaps a road to heaven nearby?
In my dream, I roam in white clouds.

13. WANG WEI (701–761)

SENDING OFF A FRIEND RETURNING TO THE MOUNTAINS

This mountain man is returning,
The clouds dark *ming ming*, the rain fierce *fei fei*,.
In the river, the waves raging, green reeds flat,
The white egret suddenly gets up and flies away.
My friend, don't step into the water, raising your robe,
Ten thousand mountains, one after another, and a lone cloud floating.
Heaven and earth, hard to distinguish,
The trees dense, the air agitated,
The monkeys, out of sight, crying.
Suddenly, the evening sun is west of the mountains,
I see the east hills, a distant hamlet,
The open prairie green, stretching a thousand *li*,
Despondent, I think of you disappearing into the distance.

REPLY TO THE FRIENDS' VISIT

Ah, I am a widower,[91]
Sad, this lonely life.
Secluded in Lantian,
Tilling lean land.
At year end I pay taxes,
Make offerings to the spirits.
At sunrise, I go to the east hill,
Dew not yet dried on the grass,
At sunset, seeing the evening smoke and lights,
I come home, the tools on my shoulders.

---

[91] The poet lost his wife when he was still young, before thirty.

I hear I have visitors.
The brushwood gate is swept well enough,
But what to serve them?
Cut the melons, beat the dates off the tree.
Thus I receive these distinguished guests.
This graying man
Feels ashamed of having no fine bamboo mat,
Seats them on briar and straw rugs.
Gently, we boat on the pond,
Pick the lotus flowers,
Quietly watch the white sturgeons swim by,
Our reflections on the clear water.
The mountain birds fly away in flocks,
The sun vanishes behind light haze.
Some in carriage, some on horseback,
The guests are leaving, in a flash, like a shower passing.
The sparrows are rackety in the desolate village,
The chickens cackling in the empty yard,
Thus returns my dark solitude.
Repeatedly, I sigh in tears.

REPLY TO ZHANG SHAOFU[92]

In my old age, I just love tranquility,
Ten thousand things, no concern of mine.
To look back, no lasting plan.
Quietly,[93] I return to my old wood,
The pine wind plays with my loose sash,
The moon over the hill shines on my hand plucking the lute.
You ask about the art of success,
The fisherman's song sinks deep in the water.

---

[92] Shaofu is an office title, vice-magistrate of a district. Zhang Shaofu is an unknown person.
[93] The expression "*kong ru*" refers to a quiet state of mind, free of all thoughts, in a Buddhist sense.

SHIMEN TEMPLE IN LANTIAN SHAN

Sunset, the mountains and rivers are beautiful,
I let my boat sail by the wind,
Enjoying the view, I forget the distance,
Eventually reaching the source of the river.
From far I loved the trees standing in the clouds,
At first, I wondered about the water's course,
Not knowing the clear water was turning around
To the front side of the mountain.
Leaving the boat, I carry my light cane,
Indeed, it's the right place.
Old monks, four or five,
On a stroll under the pine trees.
The morning service, before sunrise in the woods,
The night *chan*, the mountains ever stiller.
The Buddha mind reaches the shepherds,
About worldly matters, ask the woodcutters.
Nightfall, I stay by the tall trees,
Burn incense, I lie on a jade-clean floor.
The fragrance from the stream permeating my clothes,
The moon over the mountain shines on the stone wall.
I fear I might get lost on my next visit.
Sunrise tomorrow, I shall climb further to explore.
Smiling, I bid farewell to the monks.
When the flowers bloom red, I shall visit again.

AUTUMN EVENING AT THE MOUNTAIN COTTAGE

The mountain desolate after the new rain,
Evening approaching, the autumn sky.
The bright moon shines between the pines and cypresses,
The clear spring water flows over the stones.
The bamboos rustling, the washing women are gone,
The lotus flowers moving, the fishing boats have passed.
At will scatter the spring flowers.
This is where this princeling[94] shall gladly stay.

VISIT AT CUI XINGZONG'S FOREST COTTAGE[95]

The green trees, the dark foliage, cover the four surroundings,
The blue moss, growing thicker day by day, free of dust.
No cap on, your two legs stretched out, under the pine tree,
You look askance at the worldly ones.

COTTAGE IN ZHONGNAN SHAN

In my thirties, I was much devoted to Dao.[96]
Later, I lived near Zhongnan Shan.
I would go up the hill alone whenever I felt the urge,
Things of joy one knows immediately.
A walk led me to where the stream disappeared,
I sat down to watch the rising clouds.
By chance an old woodsman came by,
We talked and laughed, without thinking of leaving.

REPLY TO ZHANG YIN

This thatched cottage in Zhongnan
Faces Zhongnan Shan.
All year long no visitors, the gate locked,
All day long, the mind free of thoughts. Peace.
Nothing would hinder us drinking wine and fishing,
Could you just come to walk around together?

---

[94] Refers to the poet himself.
[95] Cui Xingzong was the poet's cousin, who lived in Zhongnan Shan, where
Wang Wei also had his cottage.
[96]. "Dao" may be read to refer to Buddhism, in view of the fact that Wang Wei
was a devout Buddhist.

HUAZIGANG HILL

Birds are flying away, no end,
The mountain chain again in autumn colors.
I climb up and down the Huazigang Hill,
When will my melancholy thoughts go away?

DEER PARK

The mountain desolate, no man in sight,
Only faint talking voices.
Late sunlight penetrates the deep forest,
Shining on the green moss.

LUANJIALAI BROOK

Sa sa, light autumn rain falling,
Water rushes down the rock-strewn creek,
Rippling, dancing, splashing.
A white egret, startled, flies up and down again.

WHITE STONE SHOAL

White Stone Shoal crystalline, shallow,
The green reeds are ready to be bundled.
The houses, east and west of the river,
Women are washing fine silk under the bright moon.

COTTAGE IN A BAMBOO GROVE

Alone sitting in the hushed bamboo grove,
I strum the lute, sing a long tune softly.
This deep wood nobody knows,
The bright moon visits, shining in.

XINYIWU[97]

Lotus flowers are on the magnolia branches,
On this mountain, the red petals have opened.
The house by the stream, still, no man around,
How dazzling they bloom and fall.

RETURNING TO SONG SHAN

The clear river escorts the endless vegetation,
The carriages and horses are gone. Peace.
The water flows as if with an aim of its own,
Dusk, birds are returning in flocks.
The abandoned rampart overlooking the old river-crossing,
The setting sun floods the autumn mountain.
The foot of Song Shan hazy far below,
Having returned, for now I keep the world shut out.[98]

RETURNING TO THE WANGCHUAN COTTAGE[99]

The bell shakes the valley intermittently,
Fewer and fewer fishermen and woodcutters.
Twilight in the distant mountains,
Alone I return, heading to the white clouds.
Water-chestnut vines, frail, struggle to stay still,
Willow blossoms, light, readily fly away.
The east shore, the grass in spring colors,
Wistfully, I shut my brushwood gate.

---

[97] The title means "magnolia dike," probably the name of a hill.
[98] This final line ends in the text with *bi guan* ("latch the door"), which means
in Daoist parlance withdrawal from the worldly life.
[99] The poet's cottage in Lantian Xian, southeast of the capital (Changan).

AT THE MOUNTAIN COTTAGE

Stillness, I shut the brushwood gate.
The limitless blue, I watch the setting sun's glow.
Cranes' nests in the pine trees everywhere,
Visitors rarely enter this thatch gate.
The green bamboos have put on their fresh powder,
The red lotuses have shed their old garments.
At the river-crossing, lights have begun to appear.
Here and there water chestnut pickers are returning.

JOY OF THE GARDEN

The peach red still drenched in the night's rain,
The willow green still clad in spring mist.
The flowers on the ground, the boy hasn't yet swept,
The orioles singing, the mountain guest is still asleep.

TRANQUILITY AT THE WANGCHUAN COTTAGE

Ever since my return to White Village,[100]
I haven't gone back to Blue Gate.[101]
Often leaning to the tree before the eaves,
I gaze at the hamlet far away on the plain.
The wild rice patch, green, reflecting on the water,
The white swans turn their wings, heading to the mountains.
In stillness, this Yuling Zi[102],
Carrying water from the sweep, irrigates his garden,

---

[99] The poet's cottage in Lantian Xian, southeast of the capital (Changan).
[100] Refers to the Wangchuan Cottage.
[101] Refers to Changan, the capital.
[102] Yuling Zi, a recluse during the Warring States period, who is said to have worked as a serf in the field in order to avoid serving for the king of Chu. The poet is referring to himself.

DURING A RAINY SPELL AT THE WANGCHUAN COTTAGE

During the rainy spell, in this hushed wood, the cooking smoke
    hesitantly rises,
Steam goosefoot leaves, boil millet, bring them to the east field.
Over the hazy paddies fly white egrets,
In the dense summer forest, yellow orioles chirp.
In the mountain, I practice stillness, watching morning hibiscus,
Under a pine tree, I cleanse the mind, picking hollyhock.
This old farmer[103] no longer plays seat-fight with others,[104]
Why do the gulls still doubt him[105]?

A FARM HOUSE BY THE WEI RIVER

The slanting sunlight shines on the desolate hamlet,
Cows and sheep are returning on the narrow village alley.
An old farmer, waiting for his herdboy,
Leans on his cane by the twig door.
Pheasants' call, wheat seedlings tall,
Silkworms asleep,[106] mulberry leaves all but gone.
A farmer comes by, carrying his hoe on his shoulder,
Meeting, the two farmers chat amiably.
Envious of their carefree life,
Wistfully, I sing "Shi Wei".[107]

---

[103] Refers to the poet himself.

[104] "Seat-fight" refers to an episode in *Lie Zi* (Ch. 2), in which Yang Zhu does seat-grabbing with his fellow guests in an inn. But one may read it in its plain sense, meaning the position-seeking of public life.

[105] This line also refers to an episode in *Lie Zi* (Ch. 2). In the story, a man who loves seagulls and plays with them, one day goes out to the beach with the intention of catching one of them for a meal for his father, who had wished it, and discovers that none of them would come close to him, while flying over his head.

[106] Indicates the silkworms' sloughing stage.

[107] The title of a song in the *Shi Jing*. The first two lines of the song: "How have you declined/ Why not return?" These two lines are repeated in the second of the two-stanza song.

PASSING XIANGJI TEMPLE

Not knowing where Xiangji Temple is,
I climb several *li* to the cloud-clad peak.
Ancient trees, no human trail,
Deep in the mountain, whence that peal of the bell?
A rivulet from a spring chokes through precipitous rocks,
Sunlight cool on green pines.
Twilight at the corner of a quiet pool,
A monk in peaceful meditation, quelling deadly dragons.[108]

FAREWELL

Dismount from the horse, I offer you a farewell drink.
Where are you heading to? I ask.
You say the world is not for you,
You are withdrawing to the foot of the South Mountain.
Go, I will not ask another question,
There you will never be without white clouds.

A SCENE AT THE OUTSKIRTS OF LIANGZHOU

Only three houses, belonging to an old farmer,
Few neighbors in this frontier village.
In progress is a shaman dance at the village shrine,
Flute and drum accompanying, thanksgiving to the rice-field spirit.
The shaman pours wine, soaking a straw dog,
Burns incense, prostrates before the wood man.
She flittingly dances again and again,
Her silk footwear raising dust.

---

[108] Meaning illusory thoughts.

AT PEI DI'S SMALL TERRACE[109]

Quiet life, you never leave home,
Cloud-clad mountains filling your eyes.
The setting sun goes down where birds vanish,
The autumn plain in peace, away from all humanity.
Far away the edge of the distant forest, you know well,
None will see your eaves.
Welcome visitors come, often riding the moonlight,
Gatekeeper, don't lock the gate.

SEND-OFF

In this mountain, having sent off a visitor,
I close the brushwood gate. Sundown.
The spring grass green year after year,
Will this princeling return, or not?

FAREWELL TO THE WANGCHUAN COTTAGE

Slowly moves my carriage,
Sadly I ride through the pine forest, vines riotous.
I can bear farewell to the green mountains,
But how can I part with the emerald water?

IN THE MOUNTAIN

Jing Xi Creek bares its white stones,
The sky cold, red leaves sparse.
Lately, no rain on this mountain path,
Yet the green of the air wets the hiker's robe.

---

[109] Pei Di is a close friend of the poet. The two often composed poems, rhyming
with each other's verse.

16. LI BAI (701–762)

ALONE SITTING IN JINGTING SHAN

Flying high, all the birds have vanished,
The lone cloud too, gone. Peace.
Only with Jingting Shan
I never get tired, looking at each other.

WHITE HERON

A white heron alights on the autumn water,
Alone, like frost falling,
In peace, it remains there a while,
Standing by itself on the shoal.

THINKING OF THE EAST HILL

For long I haven't gone to the East Hill,
How many times have the roses bloomed there,
And white clouds returned to scatter away?
On whose house does the bright moon go down?

SONGS OF QIUPU

(5)
The shore of Qiupu, a family of white monkeys
Jumping, vaulting, like snow flying,
One pulls down a baby from a tree branch,
Playfully drinks the moon from the water.

(13)
The crystalline water cleanses the white moon,
The moon bright, a white egret flies away.

The youngsters listen to the girls picking water chestnuts,
Together in moon light, they return home singing.

(15)
This white hair three thousand feet
Is so long due to my melancholy.
I don't know what's inside this clear mirror,[110]
Whence the autumn frost of the shore?

QUESTION-ANSWER IN THE MOUNTAIN

Why do you live in a green mountain? asks someone.
I laugh without answering, my mind at ease.
Peach blossoms floating, the mountain stream flows on and on.
Another universe altogether, not man's.

GAZE AT THE LU SHAN WATERFALL

The sun shines on Xiang Lu Peak, purple haze rising,
In the distance I see the waterfall, a great river hanging.
The flying stream descends straight three thousand feet,
One wonders if the Milky Way is falling from the Ninth Heaven.

GAZE AT TIANMEN SHAN

Tianmen Shan splitting in the middle, the Yangzi opens wide,
The blue water, flowing eastward, turns straight north.
From both shores the green mountains jut out, facing each other,
There, lone sail comes down, bathing in the sun's glow.

---

[110] Refers to the water surface.

AT THE JINLING PHOENIX TERRACE

The phoenix played on the Phoenix Terrace,
Gone is the phoenix, the terrace empty, alone the Yangzi flows on.
The palace of the Wu, the grass buries the hushed paths,
The nobles of the Jin, their fineries now in the old mounds.
Three mountains[111] half beyond the blue sky,
One river[112] divides, the White Egret Islet in the middle.
The floating clouds covering the sun,
Changan, out of view, makes me sad.

SEND OFF DU FU AT THE STONE GATE

Our farewell drinking, already how many days?
Climbing to the terraces, sauntering by the ponds.
When shall we, at the Stone Gate,
Open a wine jug once again?
The autumn waves low on the Si River,
The sea blue lights up Culai Shan.
Flying tumbleweeds, we go each his way.
For now, let us dry up the cups in our hands.

SENDING OFF A FRIEND

The green mountains stretch north of the city,
The white river circles the east city-wall.
Once we part at this place,
A lone tumbleweed, you will travel ten thousand *li*.
A floating cloud is the wanderer's mind,
The sinking sun, the friend's heart.
We leave here, waving,
Sadly, the parting horses neighing.

---

[111] Southwest of Jinling. the present-day Nanjing.
[112] Refers to the Yangji.

SEND OFF A FRIEND TO SHU

You hear the road of Shu is so precipitous, hard to go,
The cliff rising in front of your face,
The clouds by the horse's head.
But the fragrant trees surround the hanging bridges,
The spring river circles Chengdu,
Man's rise and fall in life already fixed,
There is no need to ask Junping.[113]

SEND OFF MENG HAORAN AT HUANG HAO PAVILION

You travel east, leaving Huang Hao Pavilion,
Third Month, mist and flowers, you go down to Yangzhou.
The lone sail vanishing to the blue sky,
I see only the Yangzi flow away to the horizon.

SONG OF THE QINGXI RIVER

The Qingxi cleans my mind,
Its color unlike other rivers.
One wonders if at the Xinan River
You could see its bottom like this.
The passers-by walk in the bright mirror,
Birds fly crossing the picture screen.
Dusk approaching, the monkeys yowl,
Far from home this traveler sinks deep in nostalgia.

STAY OVER BY THE QINGXI RIVER

Night arriving, I stay over by the Qingxi River,
The inn behind the blue cliff.

---

[113] For divination. See p. 55, n81.

By the eaves hangs the Great Bear on the post.
By the pillow the sounds of the stream and wind.
As the moon sinks behind the western mountain,
Jiu jiu, the night monkeys start to cry.

GAZE AT THE LU SHAN WATERFALL

Climb to the Xiang Lu Peak from the west,
View the waterfall in the south.
The river hangs three hundred *zhang*,[114]
Spews water down the gorge several tens of *li*.
Sudden illumination, as if by lightning,
Darkness, as if about to raise a white rainbow.
First, I wondered if the Milky Way had fallen,
Its half flowing out from the cloud-covered sky.
As I look up, it comes down ever mightier,
How stupendous the work of the Creator!
The wind from the sea fails to interrupt its fall,
The moon over the Yangzi shines on it in vain.
In the air, the water in turmoil, spattering, splattering,
Washes down the blue walls, left and right.
The flying pearls scatter, the light mist forming,
The falling foams boil over huge rocks.
Thus, I have enjoyed this majestic mountain.
Facing it, my mind ever more contented,
Don't speak of just rinsing the mouth with this heavenly fluid,
Also, wash your dust-covered face clean.
This place, indeed, so in tune with my likings,
I wish to leave the human realm forever.

DRINK ALONE UNDER THE MOON

Between the flowers, a jar of wine,
Alone I drink. No friends.

---

[114] 1 *zhang* about 10 feet long.

Raise the cup to the moon,
Sitting with my shadow, a party of three.
The moon, of course, doesn't know drinking,
The shadow merely follows me.
For a while, shadow and moon in company,
Fun. Spring must be enjoyed.
I sing, the moon roams,
I dance, the shadow scrambles.
Awake, we enjoy our company,
Once drunk, we scatter, each his way.
This unfeeling play, our bond will never end.
Let us promise, we shall meet again in the Milky Way.

A NIGHT WITH A FRIEND

Wash away the old sorrows of a millennium,
I stay on with a friend, drinking a hundred jars of wine.
Pleasant evening, our talk fittingly cool.
The moon shining white, I am unable to sleep.
Drunk, lying in this empty mountain,
Heaven and earth my beddings.

ON THE WALL OF YUAN DANQIU'S MOUNTAIN HERMITAGE

My friend, you live on the East Hill,
Loving the beauty of hills and glens.
In verdant spring you lie in the empty wood,
In broad daylight you are still in bed.
Pine wind cleans your clothes,
The stony pool cleanses your mind.
I envy you resting on a high pillow in the emerald mist,
No bustling noise of the world.

VISITING YUAN DANQIU IN THE MOUNTAIN

Unannounced I make a visit to Yuan Danqiu's hermitage
On impulse, unaware of the distance.
The green cliff beyond a stream hard to wade through,
Daylight about to turn dark.
I have barely climbed three or four hills,
Yet made hundreds of turns.
In stillness I hear monkeys yowl,
I see the clouds rise one by one.
The beautiful moon appears over the pines,
The clear autumn air fills the hollow glen.
Old snow in a deep ravine,
Cold spring water runs down through rock crevices.
Peaks thrust into the mid-sky,
From which one may enjoy an unhindered view.
Danqui's calling voice from afar,
Seeing me, he is laughing.
At last, I reach his deep gorge,
For the first time I know the peace of a recluse.
Joyous reunion, we stay up through the long night,
Lucent daybreak, I promise him my return.

15. CUI HAO (704–754)

HUANG HAO PAVILION

The old man[115] departed long ago, riding the white clouds,
This place empty, there stands only Huang Hao Pavilion.
The yellow crane, once gone, never returns,
The white clouds, for a thousand years, *you you* in the sky.
The air clear over the Yangzi, the trees in Hanyang[116] so
    distinctly visible,
The fragrant grass lush on the Cockatoo Islet.
Sundown. In which direction is my old village?
The mist over the ripples makes me nostalgic.

---

[115] Of the story of Huang Hao Pavilion. According to the story, an old man would frequent a certain wine house, but without paying for his drink. The owner, however, always served him kindly. Some time later, the old man came and painted on the wall a yellow crane (*huang hao*) with orange peel. He then stopped coming. Thereafter, whenever people sang drinking in the wine house, the crane on the wall would dance to the song. Ten years later, the old man came back and played the flute. Thereupon white clouds rose, and the crane flew out of the wall. The old man got on the bird's back and flew away, riding on the white clouds. Later, the owner built a pavilion on the site and called it Huang Hao Lu (Yellow Crane Pavilion).

[116] On the opposite shore.

16. CHANG JIAN (708–765)

ON THE WALL OF THE *CHAN* HALL BEHIND POSHAN SI TEMPLE

Clear morning, I enter the old temple,
Early sun shining over the tall forest.
A winding path leads to the hushed place,
The *chan* hall deep in the thicket of flowers and trees.
The mountain in sunlight delights the birds' nature,
The cool light on the water pool cleanses man's mind empty.
All sounds stilled,
Only the bells and chimes resounding in the air.

17. CHU GUANGXI (707–759?)

ANGLING AT AN INLET

Springtime, I cast a fishing line in the green inlet.
Spring far advanced, wildly apricot flowers fall.
The crystalline water, one questions its shallowness,
The lotuses moving, one knows fish are scattering.
At dusk, expecting my dear one,
I fasten my boat to the shore by the green willow trees.

TO MOUNTAIN MAN SUN

The trees fresh green, Second Month, a lone boat returns,
The river full of clear water, flowers covering the hill.
Let me ask you, mountain man,
Would you sometimes visit the human world?

18. QIAN QI (710–780)

TO THE RETURNING GEESE

Xiao Xiang,[117] isn't this place good enough for you?
   Why are you leaving?
Water green, sand bright, shores moss-covered.
Moon-lit night, the sound of the twenty-five-stringed lute,
That clear sadness unbearable. I am returning.

---

[117] This refers to the southern part of Dongting Lake, where the Xiao and Xiang, two rivers, come together.

19. DU FU (712–770)

BALLAD OF WAR-WAGONS

Wagons rumbling, horses whinnying,
Men on the march, bows and arrows at their waists.
Dads, moms, wives, children sending them off, running along,
Dust cloud, the Xinyang Bridge no more visible.
They wail, pulling at the men's clothes, stamping their feet,
    blocking the road,
The wailing voices rise straight up, swirling the clouds.
A passer-by asks the marching men,
Repeated call-ups, they say only.
Some, sent north at fifteen for the defense of the Yellow River,
Are now serving at garrison farms in the west.
When they left, the village chiefs gave them head-wraps,[118]
After returning white-haired, they are again called to
    guard the border.
In the frontier blood flows making a sea,
Yet Emperor Wu[119] has not given up his desire to open
    the frontier land.
In the two hundred districts of Shandong, haven't you heard,
Brambles and weeds are growing in the ten thousand villages?
Sturdy women may grab plow and hoe,
Grains grow without order in the field.
Besides, those soldiers from Shanxi, who fight tough battles
Are driven like dogs and chickens.

---

[118] Probably as part of the rite of passage.

[119] On the surface, the ballad refers to the reign of Wu Di of the Han, who repeatedly launched military campaigns for territorial expansion in the northwest, the northeast and the south. However, Du Fu is in fact criticizing the frontier policies of Emperor Xuanzong of the Tang, which called for a continuous mobilization for military engagements in the border regions during the poet's own time.

Although you ask us, sir,
How could we draftees dare express grievances?
This winter, for instance,
The Shanxi soldiers were given no leave at all.
Government officials suddenly levied taxes,
From what could people pay taxes?
Indeed, I realize it's bad to produce boys,
Better to produce girls instead.
Girls may be married off to neighbors,
But boys will be buried in the company of weeds.
Don't you know that in Qinghai
From of old, nobody takes care of white bones?
New ghosts lamenting, old ghosts wailing,
When the sky is dark and drizzling, you hear their sobbing sounds.

SENDING OFF GAO SHI[120]

At Kongdong Shan, wheat is ripe,
I wish all soldiers be given leave.
May I tell you to ask your general,
Why must the army be sent to this end of the world?
A falcon, as though it had not yet had its full of meat,
Spreads its wings and flies up, following its master's command.
Gao Shi, astride on a saddled horse,
You look like a knight-errant of You Bing.[121]
You have pulled yourself out of the lowly county clerk office,
For the first time, dropping whips and sticks.
Let me ask you what office you hold
To head to Wuwei in this heat? You may answer,
Being a government official, I'm ashamed to say,
People know me as a defender of the country.
It's truly difficult to know a man,
Besides, one must be careful in conduct.

---

[120] A poet, five years senior to Du Fu.
[121] You Zhou and Bing Zhou, both places known for their knights-errant.

In ten years, you will leave your headquarters,
Perhaps, carrying your own banner.
This appointment is already a big promotion,
You may well be satisfied.
A man's achievement in public life
Also comes in his old age.
I always hate to see my friendship go shallow.
You and I will be at the opposite edges of the sky,
Never meeting, like Orion and Scorpio.
Can can, my sadness hurts deep inside.
The gust blows away a large goose,
It's impossible to pursue it.
Yellow dust darkens the desert,
I wonder when you will return.
At the frontier fort, if you still have strength,
Send me quickly your war poem.

DRUNKEN SONG

All high officials, one by one, are showing up at their ministries,
Professor Zheng of Guangwen[122] is alone cold in his office.
In their mansions, the ministers feast sumptuously,
The professor is short on food.
The professor's philosophy derives from Fu Xi,[123]
His talents excel those of Qu Yuan and Song Yu.[124]
His virtue worthy of a generation's respect, yet he is
    constantly strapped,
His name may last for ages, but who knows for what use?

---

[122] In his note to the title of this poem Du Fu writes: "Dedicated to Zheng Qian, Doctor of Guangwen Guan." Guangwen Guan was an institute attached to Guozi Jian, the department of the highest learning.
[123] I.e.., Fu Xi Shi, one of the three mythical kings of China in ancient tradition He was believed to have taught Chinese people such things as farming and fishing as well as the Chinese script and the eight diagrams of the *Yi Jing* (Book of Change).
[124] Both poets of Chu during the Warring States period.

This rustic of Duling[125] is worse, I am a laughingstock,
My rags short and hard to put limbs through, my sideburns
 as flimsy as thread.
Daily I buy five pecks of rice from the government granary,
At times I go to Professor Zheng to share my aspirations.
As soon as I have money, I seek him,
I buy wine without a second thought.
Forgetting propriety, I begin to talk to him as if we are buddies,
Heavy drink truly my master.
Clear night, stillness deepening, we keep pouring spring wine,
Fine rain before the lantern, flowers falling under the eaves.
But I feel spirits stirring as we loudly sing,
How would I care if I fill the ditch dead from starvation?
Xiangru,[126] though a rare genius, washed the dishes,
Ziyun,[127] the scholar of scripts, finally threw himself from a balcony.
Professor, compose soon your "Oh, Let Me Return",[128]
Your rock-strewn field is wild, your thatched cottage moss-covered.
Confucian scholarship, what good is it for us?
Confucius and Robber Zhi[129] both turned to dust.
Hearing of this, don't fall into depression,
As long as we meet in this life, let us fill our cups.

SONG OF EIGHT DRINKING IMMORTALS

Zhizhang on horseback sways, as though on a boat,
Flowers before his eyes,[130] he falls into a well, falls asleep
 at the bottom.
Ruyang, three bushels before the morning audience,
On the street, meeting a malt wagon, drips saliva.

---

[125] Refers to the poet himself. Du Fu lived near Duling.
[126] Sima Xiangru, a poet and scholar of the Han dynasty.
[127] Yang Xiong, a philosopher during the Han dynasty, known for his knowledge of ancient scripts.
[128] Tao Yuanming's "Oh, Let Me Return."
[129] Or Dao Zhi. See *The Zhuang Zi* (e.g. Ch . 29).
[130] This phrase (*yan hua*) is commonly taken to mean "dazed."

He regrets being not enfeoffed to the Wine Spring.
Li Shizhi daily spends ten thousand coins for entertainment,
Drinks like a whale swilling a hundred rivers.
Cup to his mouth, he declares his preference of blissful holiness
  over wise sagehood.
Cui Zongzhi, cool and handsome,
Raising the cup, his white eyes gaze[131] at the blue sky,
Shining bright, as though a jade tree in wind.
Su Jin fasts long before the embroidered Buddha,
When drunk, frequently he loves to escape into the *chan* state.
Li Bai, one bushel, a hundred poems,
When in Changan, he is deep asleep in a wine house.
When called to the palace, he finds no footing to go on board.
He calls himself a drinking immortal.
Zhang Xu, after three cups, a holy calligrapher,
No cap, bare head, before a king or prince.
His brush at work on paper, as though mist rising.
Jiao Sui, five bushels, profound talk,
So outstanding, his eloquence surprises all present.

VILLAGE OFFICIAL OF SHIHAO

After dusk I stay at Shihao Village,
At night, an official comes to arrest the man of the house.
The old man escapes over the wall,
The old woman goes out the gate to see the official.
The man's shouting, how angry,
The woman's crying, how terrified!
I see her step forward and plead,
Our three sons are gone to defend Yecheng,
One of them sends us a letter by someone,
Two of them have recently been killed.
We, survivors, for a while may hang onto life,
But the dead are forever gone.

---

[131] Meaning looking askance.

In this house, there is no one else,
Only our grandson, still milk-drinking,
His mother still around,
Has no decent skirt to wear to go out.
This old one, though frail,
I beg you to take me with you tonight.
If you send me at once to Heyang to serve,
I might be able to help with breakfast cooking.
A long night, her voice no more,
I hear someone sobbing.
After sunrise, I am on the road again,
Bidding farewell to the old man alone.

DREAM OF LI BAI, two poems

(1)
When separate by death, you swallow your voice in time,
When separate in life, your sadness never goes away.
The south of the Yangzi, the land of malaria,
No news from my friend there in exile.
This man appears in my dream,
Clearly I have for long thought of him.
To my surprise, in the dream he isn't his usual soul.
He comes a long way, an immeasurable distance,
From the maple leaves green,
Returns to the garrison post black.
You are now caught in the net,
How have you managed to fly out?
The moon, going down, fills the rafters of this room,
I doubt if it shines on your face.
The water deep, the waves flooding,
Don't let the dragons prey on you.

(2)
Floating clouds go away all day,
The man on the road never arrives.
Three nights I keep dreaming of you.

Our friendship so close, I see your feelings.
Announcing your leaving, you get fidgety.
Apologetically, you say, Coming is not easy,
Winds and waves unceasing in this region of rivers and lakes,
The rudder may fall off.
Leaving the gate, you once scratched your white hair,
As though you gave up your life ambition.
Tall caps and covered carriages fill the gorgeous capital,
This man alone, gaunt and worn out.
Who says the meshes of the heavenly net large?
This man, near old age, is tangled in the net,
Your famous name for ten thousand years,
But stillness, nothing after you are gone.

ON THE WALL OF ZHANG SHI'S HERMITAGE

This spring mountain I climb alone to visit you,
Ding ding, the sound of felling trees deepens its still.
The path along the creek, cold from the icy snow in the gully,
The evening sun over the Stone Gate shines on the wooded hill.
Free of a seeking mind, you recognize the breath of gold and silver
    at night.
Far from a harming mind, you observe deer at play in the morning.
Having come on an urge, I am in the dark, at a loss where to go.
As I sit with you, it's as though facing an empty boat afloat.

SPRING VIEW

The country in ruin,[132] the hills and rivers as ever,
Springtime in the city, grass and trees grow rank.
Lamenting the time, tears at the sight of flowers,
My heart, saddened from separations, startles at the birds' rustling.
Beacons burning for three months on end,
Words from home are as precious as ten thousand pieces of gold.

---

[132] Due to An Lu Shan's rebellion.

My white hair getting thinner from scratching,
It barely holds a hairpin.

SITTING WITH WINE AT THE QUJIANG RIVER[133]

Outside the royal estate by the river, I sit alone, without leaving,
The crystal palace glistening more than ever.
The peach flowers fall one by one, following the willow catkins,
The yellow birds[134] fly up with white birds, again and again.
I have been given to drink for sometime, avoiding others,
    they have abandoned me.
Indifferent at work, I have been out of tune with the world.
I am again longing for the Blue Sea far away,
This old man, merely suffering inside, hasn't taken off his
    official robe.

SOUND OF THE FLUTE AT NIGHT

The sound of the flute, autumn mountains, breeze, clear moon,
Who is playing it so beautifully? Heart-rending!
The wind carries the melody so exquisite, its yin-yang in
    perfect harmony.
The moon by the mountain pass illumines several peaks.
The horsemen from the north, in the middle of night,
    would retreat,[135]
I think of the Wuling piece played during Ma Yuan's
    south campaign.[136]
Back home, now the willows in the yard may be losing their leaves,
How can I revive them in my melancholy thought?

---

[133] The river that flows by the south-east corner of the Changan city-wall.
[134] I.e., orioles.
[135] Saddened by the sound of the flute.
[136] During his military expedition to the south, General Ma Yuan (of the Late Han) had one of his men play the flute at his camp at the riverside.

JADE FLOWER PALACE [137]

The creek flows around the palace, pine breeze ceaseless,
A gray rat scurries under the old tiles,
Not knowing what the royal palace is.
The remains of the structure below the cliff,
The dark rooms, ghost-fire blue.
The paths corroded, sobbing streams.
The ten thousand sounds, truly coming from *sheng wu*? [138]
So clear this autumn scenery!
The beauties turn to dirt,
All the more so those ugly made-up faces.
Of the escorts that accompanied the golden carriage,
Alone the stone horses have survived.
Despondent, sitting on the grass,
I sing aloud, tears in the eyes.
Time marching on relentlessly,
Who will live on forever?

TRAVEL TO THE NORTH

[Du Fu wrote this famous poem during the An Lu Shan rebellion. The capital city, Changan, was still in the hands of the rebels. He had escaped from his brief captivity in the city, and rejoined the new emperor, Su Zong in Fengxiang. His family had fled to Luzhou, far north. In this poem, Du Fu visits them there, meeting them for the first time since their separation.

One may read this long poem (altogether 140 lines) in three parts, of which only the middle part (lines 21–93) describes his reunion with the family, while the other two are devoted to his thought of gratitude and loyalty to the emperor during this time of turmoil. Translated here is only the middle part.]

---

[137] North of Changan.
[138] *Sheng* and *yu*, both woodwind instruments.

Slowly I trudge on and on along the footpaths in fields
    and rice paddies,
Bleak smoke rises over desolate villages at distance.
What meets my eyes are mostly war scars,
People moaning and bleeding.
I look back to Fengxiang,
Banners and flags flapping in the evening sky.
Walking on, I climb the cold mountains, one after another,
Often looking for waterholes for the horses.
The Bin Basin, sunken in low ground,
The Jin River swelling in the middle.
Before me there stands a tiger fierce-looking,
Whose roaring may shatter the blue cliff.
The chrysanthemums hang their autumn flowers,
Rocks on the ruts from the old wheels.
The clouds in the blue sky arouse my spirit,
The mountain solitude can also be delightful.
The wild berries everywhere so lovely,
Mixed with chestnut oak acorns,
Some red, like cinnabar,
Some black, like lacquer.
Rain and dew nourishing,
All plants, sweet or bitter, bear their fruit,
Fancifully, I think of the Peach Land.[139]
All the more, I lament my time of misfortune.
Over the rolling hills, I see the altar ground of Luzhou,
Hills and ravines, alternately, rising and sinking,
I am already down here, walking along the stream,
When my servant is still up there between trees.
An owl cries on a yellowing mulberry tree,
Field mice scrounge around the scattered holes.
Late at night, I pass by a battlefield,
The cold moon shining on white bones.
Those million troops at Tongguan last year,
Why did they flee so quickly?

---

[139] Paradise.

Eventually, bringing a half the Qin population
Under attack to be lost.
Not to speak of me, who fell in the rebels' hands,
Escaping, I found myself, hair all grey,
A year gone, I arrive at this thatch-roofed hut.
Wife and children, in rags, a hundred patches,
Wailing, over the pine's rustling,
The sad spring trickles quietly, sobbing along.
My beloved son,
His face so pale, whiter than snow,
Seeing his father, turns away, crying.
Dirt all over, no socks on his feet.
In front of the bed are my two daughters,
The patched clothes barely cover their knees.
The sea scene, the waves cut in pieces,
The embroidered figures all crooked and damaged.
Tianwu and Zifeng[140] are
Upside down, in tatters.
My feelings distressed,
I become sick in bed for several days, vomiting.
Of course, my travel bag contains gifts,
Things to relieve my family of their cold misery.
Also talcum powder and eyebrow paint in the package.
I display them on bed.
My thin wife, instantly light on her face,
The silly girls quickly straighten their hair with combs.
They never fail to do what they learn from their mother.
In the morning, they put on powder wherever they can,
Eventually, smearing red and black all over,
An utter mess, making their eyebrows huge.
I have come alive to meet these children,
It's as though I have forgotten my hunger and thirst.
They pull my beard to ask something,
But who could be mad and scold them?

---

[140] Both mythological creatures mentioned in the *Shanhai Jing*. (See p. 48, n74). Tianwu is a sea deity with human face and tiger-like body, and Zifeng a purple phoenix.

Remembering my sadness in the rebels' hands,
I would gladly tolerate their misbehavior, however naughty.
Coming home, I thus console myself,
But of our livelihood what can I say?

SENDING OFF A FRIEND FAR

Men in armor everywhere in this land,
For what are you on this long journey?
Your dear ones and friends all wailing,
You ride off on horseback, leaving this desolate town.
Grass and trees late in the year,
The Yellow River at the frontier deep in frost and snow.
Was it already yesterday that we sent you off?
So I see the meaning of the old poem.[141]

QINZHOU, twenty poems[142]

(1)
All that meet my eyes are sad scenes of life,
Thanks to my acquaintances I have made this long journey.
I cross Long Pass by slow trails, trembling,
Reaching the frontier post, sadness overcomes me.
Night by the Yulong River, the water low,
Autumn on Niaoshu Shan, deserted.
Coming west, I inquire about the fighting,
My spirit broken, I go no further, will stay here.

---

[141] This refers to a poem by Jiang Yan of Liang (6th cent.), in which the poet
sadly recalls "It is as if yesterday that I sent you off." However, the meaning of
the line unclear. The penultimate line seems to suggest that the poet wrote this
poem the day after sending off the traveler.
[142] Qinzhou, located in Gansu, is the place to which Du Fu moved with his
family during the severe famine of 759 in Shanxi.

(3)

The sounds of drums and horns in the frontier counties,
Night approaches over the open plain.
The sounds in the autumn sky, rising from the great earth,
Scatter in the wind, sadly die away into the clouds.
Hugging leaves, the cold cicadas quiet,
A lone bird is late returning to the hill.
The sounds spread in all ten thousand directions,
Where would my road lead to in the end?

AT TONGGU, seven poems[143]

(1)

Traveler, traveler, his name Zimei,[144]
White head, disheveled hair falling below the ears.
Year after year, he gathers acorns, following after monkeys,
The air cold, dusk in the mountain valley.
No word from the Central Plain,[145] no way to return home,
Hands and legs frozen, chapped, skin and muscle numb.
Ah, the first song sung, already sad!
A wind pitying me comes from the sky.

(2)

Long hoe, long hoe, white wooden handle!
I trust my existence to you, you are my life!
No *huangjing*[146] shoots in the snow-covered mountain,
My robe, so short, won't cover the shins, though I pull it repeatedly.
This time, I come home with you empty-handed,
The boys are groaning, the girls whining, the four walls still.

---

[143] Du Fu moves from Qinzhou to Tonggu.

[144] Zimei is Du Fu's courtesy name (*zi*).

[145] Where the capital is. Du Fu comes from this region.

[146] *Polygonatum*, a member of the lily family. The plant's underground stem is used in Chinese medicine. In the poem, Du Fu is in the mountain searching for *huangjing* with his "long hoe," presumably, to sell.

Ah, the second song, I let it out at last.
The neighbors put on sorrowful faces for me.

A GUEST ARRIVES

For years I have been suffering from asthma,
Recently I have chosen our house facing the river.[147]
Far from the bustling, mean world,
Relaxed and pleasant, most suitable for me.
A guest stops by this thatched house,
I call my child to straighten his cap of grass cloth.
Sparse are vegetable sprouts in the plot I till myself,
I pick a few of them to treat him cordially.

RIVERSIDE VILLAGE

The clear river flows around the village, hugging it,
Long summer in this riverside village, all quiet.
The swallows flying back and forth freely over the house,
The gulls congregating fraternally on the water.
My old wife draws a *qi*-game[148] board on paper,
My child taps at a needle to make a fish-hook.
Being sickly, I must get medicines,
Other than that, what more would I seek?

GLAD RAIN ON A SPRING NIGHT

The good rain knows its season,
Come spring, it brings forth new growths.

---

[147] Huanhua Xi, a river which flows southeast of Chengdu. Du Fu had moved to this city from Tonggu.
[148] The game commonly known by its Japanese name, *go*, which is the Japanese pronunciation of the character *qi*.

Accompanying winds, it steals into the night,
Watering all things softly, soundless.
Field paths and clouds pitch-dark,
The torches on the river boats alone lighting.
At dawn you will see pink, wet scenes,
Flowers heavy from rain in the Brocaded City.[149]

RIVERSIDE PAVILION

Flat on back, warm in the riverside pavilion,
Reciting poems slowly, I take in the country scenery.
The water flowing, my thoughts not hurried,
The clouds still, my mind also relaxed.
Ji ji, quietly this spring is about to pass,
Xin xin, joyously all things flourish, each its way.
But I cannot return to my old forest,
To get rid of my distress, I force myself to write this poem.

THOUGHT AT THE RAILING BY THE RIVER

Away from the city-wall, this house broad-beamed,
No village nearby, our view reaches far out.
The river crystalline, the shores flat and low,
The dense forest dark, many flowers bloom till late.
Fine rain falling, tiny fish appear to the surface,
In the breeze, the young swallows fly sideways.
A hundred thousand houses in the city,
A couple of houses in this place.

RETURN IN SPRING

Moss-covered path, bamboos along the river,
Thatched roof, flowers covering the ground.

---

[149] I.e., Chengdu, where the poet is staying.

Several months have passed since I left home,
Returning, there I see spring flowers unexpectedly in bloom.
Leaning on my cane, I look at the lone rock,
With a wine jar, I sit down on sands by the river.
Far out, gulls are floating on the water quietly,
Swallows, light, fly sideways in wind.
Human affairs are full of frustrations,
But my life has its limit.
This body awakes from one drunken state and goes to another,
Wherever my spirit is quickened, I make it my home.

SAILING IN A BOAT

A long sojourner in this capital of the south,[150] I till a south field.
Down-hearted, I sit by the north window, looking to the north.
During the day, I take my old wife in a small boat for sailing,
When sunny, we watch the children bathe in the clear water.
A pair of butterflies naturally chase each other,
By nature a lotus stem grows a pair of flowers abreast.
We bring with us whatever tea or sugarcane juice we happen to have,
Our earthen jars are as precious as jade vessels.

SUNSET

The setting sun on the screen hook,
By the stream, quietly spring activities go on,
Fragrant herbs in the field along the shore,
A woodcutter cooks supper in a boat by the water,
Rackety sparrows fighting fall off the branches,
Flying insects fill the garden, playing.
Unstrained wine, who discovered you?
One scoop scatters a thousand worries.

---

[150] Chengdu.

GRIEVING AT THE FALLEN CAMPHOR TREE

By the river stood a camphor tree, in front of my hut.
The village elders say, two hundred years old.
We built the hut, cutting away the reeds, all because of the tree.
Fifth Month, it sounded like cicadas singing.
A storm came from south-east, shaking the earth,
The river raged, stones flew, the clouds rushed.
The tree trunk resisted the gust, struggling,
Yet it was uprooted, heaven's doing.
Blue waves and old trees are what my nature loves,
The tree held up a lush, blue canopy on the riverside.
Farmers often stayed under it, avoiding snow and frost,
No passers-by went away without hearing its piping.
Fallen tiger, beaten dragon, it lies in company of briars,
Tears on my chest, pain in my heart.
When I compose a new poem, where would I recite it?
From now on my hut is faceless.

AUTUMN WIND DESTROYS MY THATCHED HOUSE

Eighth Month, autumn sky high, the wind, roaring angry,
Rolls up the three layers of thatch off our roof.
The thatches fly over the river, fall in the fields on the other side,
Some, hanging high on the branches in the long forest,
Some, blown low, sink in the pools by the banks.
A gang of youths from the south village, scoffing at my weak, old age,
Loot cruelly before my face, taking thatches in their arms,
And disappear into the bamboo grove.
Lips scorched, mouth dried, I am unable to shout.
Coming home, leaning on my cane, I give out deep sigh.

Soon the wind dies down, the clouds black,
The autumn sky turns twilight.
Our bedding old, cold as iron,
Our children, sleeping roughly, have torn it.
By the bedside, the ceiling leaky, no place dry,

My two legs are as thin as hemp thread, still attached.
Ever since the rebellion, I have had little sleep,
This long night, wet and moist,
How am I to get it through?
I wish I had a huge mansion of a million *jian,*
Where I could shelter all the poor literati, bringing smile to
 their faces.
No wind or rain could move it, as secure as a mountain.
Ah, when would I see before my eyes this house rise sky-high?
My hut alone in ruin, I may freeze to death. Yet, I wouldn't mind.

A FARMER SENDS ME RED CHERRIES

Cherries in the western Shu too are naturally red,
A farmer brings me a basket full of them.
As I transfer them carefully several times, I fear damaging them,
All of the tiny fruit equally round, I wonder how they can be so
 much alike.
I recall receiving the royal gifts sent to my department[151] years ago,
As I was leaving the palace,[152] I carried them most respectfully
 with both my hands.
No more gold plate and jade chopsticks,
Today I relish these new fruits, resigning myself to this life of tumble-
weed.

A CERTAIN ZHANG FROM THE OFFICE OF THE CROWN PRINCE
SENDS ME THE GIFT OF A CARPET

A visitor comes from the capital,
Gives me a gift of a green weaving.
I open the box, there rages a storm, billows surging,
In it a whale moving its tail.

---

[151] Wenxiasheng, where the emperor's decrees are deliberated.
[152] Daminggong, where the ceremony was held.

Following it is a shoal of sea creatures,
All too insignificant to be named.
The visitor says, Please use this as your carpet,
Bestow upon me the honor of presenting this for your leisure.
From your empty room, all evil spirits will run away,
Lie on it on your high pillow, and you will be clear of all afflictions
    in mind and body.
I accept your precious intent,
But I believe I am not a high official.
My keeping it, I fear, will cause me misfortune,
Its presence will bring disorder to this house of brushwood
    and brambles.
A man's clothes and furnishings determine the distinction of high
    and low,
Great is this eternal maxim!
Now I am a lowly, old man,
Beyond coarse rags I seek nothing.
This carpet is resplendent, a thing of the Palace of Pearls,
Sleeping on it will invite calamities.
I lament, the folks in government today,
In the midst of a wartime, when fighting rages everywhere,
Grab whatever power they can put their hands on,
Enjoy the life of fine clothes and fat horses.
Li Ding died in Qiyang,
Indeed, because of his arrogance.
Lai Zhen was ordered to commit suicide,
Because of his recklessness, he was quick to resort to use of force.
One hears that both of them had accumulated enormous wealth.
You can see, such conduct should invite regrettable consequences.
How can this old country man
Accept your wish to give me this valuable gift?
Rolling up the brocaded whale, I hand it back to the visitor,
At last, peace of mind.
I shake dust off the rag seat,
Feeling of shame, having served the guest goosefoot juice.

AGAIN, VISIT AT NET FISHING

Blue river, clear morning, fishermen come together,
Cast the net, pull the ropes, ten thousand fish in desperate flurry.
The skilled ones, steering the boat, quick like wind,
Crush into the waves, their poles ahead.
Small fish escape the net, not to mention,
Those in the net, half dead, half alive, gasping for breath.
Large fish, injured, their heads down,
Hardy ones, sometimes, leap from the muddy sands.
I have come to East Ferry to see the fishing for the second time.
My host, enough of sliced raw fish, again drinks.
Dusk, the dragons change their caves,
The bottom of the mountains, the sturgeons follow thunderclouds.[153]
Spears and shields, armor and horses, war never ceases.
Fenghuang and *qilin*,[154] where are they now?
My fellow men, why do you indulge in this enjoyment?
Violence to Heaven's creations saddens the sage.

FOUR PINES

The four pines barely over three feet
When I first transplanted them.
Quickly three years have passed since our separation,
Standing in pairs, they are now as tall as an adult.
I was sure to see them again, their roots undisturbed,
But didn't figure that their branches might wilt or be damaged.
Now, their colors dark, happily, their branches stretch out.
The crude hedge also thriving,
It was planted to make a small fence,
Mainly to protect the pines.
Eventually some damage,
Yet it has grown to save a thousand leaves from yellowing.

---

[153] The meaning of this and the preceding line unclear.
[154] Both mythological creatures, whose presence stands for the ideal world under the sage king: "all under heaven in peace."

I dare say I'm the owner of an old wood,
But the people of the land are still not yet in peace.
Escaping from the rebels, I am back here for the first time,
The spring grass fills my empty garden.
Watching things, I grieve at my frailty,
As I look at these pines, they console my melancholy.
A waft of fresh breeze rises and comes to me,
Touching my face like light frost.
The trees are adequate for accompanying my old age.
For now I shall wait for their canopies spreading.
My life rootless,
Uncertain is my remaining with you, my fellows.
Out of my love for you, I am writing this poem.
Let us not forget this day of our reunion,
Don't boast, in a thousand years
You will form a forest, darkening the firmament.

SLEEPLESS NIGHT

The cool of bamboo invades my bedroom,
The moon over the plain floods every corner of the yard.
Dew heavy turns into water drops,
Stars, sparse in the night sky, appear and disappear in no time.
Fireflies fly in darkness, lighting their ways,
Water birds, resting, call to one another.
Ten thousand phenomena all in the shadows of shields and spears.
Silently I grieve over the clear night passing.

TWO *JUEJU*[155]

(1)
The sun idling, the rivers and hills resplendent,
Spring breeze, flowers and grass fragrant.

---

[155] *Jueju*, a particular form of poem, consisting of four lines: two kinds, depending on whether each line has five or seven characters.

The ground thawing, swallows in the air,
The sand warm, the ducks doze off.

(2)
The river jade green, the birds whiter than ever,
The mountain green, the flowers about to inflame.
I see this spring again pass,
When will I be returning home?

NIGHT THOUGHTS ON THE ROAD[156]

Breeze over the frail grass on the shore,
The mast precarious on the lone ship sailing at night.
Stars hang low over the open plain,
The moon, rising from the water, flows down the great river.
Fame, how can I gain it by writing?
Office, I have retired from it, being old and frail.
Constantly drifting in wind, what is this like?
A beach gull afloat between heaven and earth.

AUTUMN THOUGHTS, eight poems

(1)
Jade dew wilts the maple forest,
The Wu mountain, the Wu gorge, the air desolate.
On the river the waves join the sky,
Over the fortress the clouds in the wind touch the earth, dark.
The chrysanthemums in cluster have opened again,
    another day's tears,
The lone boat moored, my heart longing for home.
Sewing winter clothes, busy with scissors and rulers everywhere,
High in Baidi City the fulling clubs[157] get faster at dusk.

---

[156] Du Fu has left Chengdu, and is sailing down the Yangzi when he writes this poem.
[157] Wooden clubs used to smooth clothing by beating it on a smooth hard surface, as if by ironing. This was an old common method of pressing cloth used in the Far East.

WHITE-LITTLE

White-little, this species of fish,
By nature two inches long.
Thin and tiny, they nourish other fishes,
People in this region eat them like salad.
Brought in store, silver flowers in jumble,
Tilt the basket, you empty snowflakes.
For their perpetuation, better leave their spawn untouched.
Take spawn and all, would it be fair?

HIKE TO THE TERRACE[158]

The wind gusty, the sky high, plaintively the monkeys cry,
The shoal clear, the sands white, the birds flying over.
The plain limitless, the tree leaves are falling *xiao xiao*,
Ceaseless the Ynagzi comes down majestically, *gun gun*.
Over ten thousand *li*, autumn sad, I am always on the road,
Sickly, year in, year out, alone I hike to the terrace.
Suffering from this hard life, frost grows on my sideburns,
Feeble, I now stay away from unstrained wine.

BALLAD OF A BOUND CHICKEN

Our boy servant is going to the market with a bound chicken to sell,
Bound tight, the chicken makes an awful complaint.
My family hates to see it eat worms and ants,
In turn, they don't think of its being cooked when sold.
Worm or chicken, which is dearer to humans?
Scolding the servant, I make him untie it.
Chicken or worm, which is to spare? Unable to answer,
I look down over the cold river, leaning to the hillside balcony.

---

[158] On the Double Ninth Day. See p. 38, n57.

DUSK

The cows and sheep are down from the hills long ago,
Every brushwood gate already closed.
Breeze and moon bring clear night,
These rivers and hills, but not my old garden.
Water from a rock spring running down the dark cliff,
Dew on grass drips to the autumn roots.
My head white in the lamplight,
Why must it busily produce sparkling flowers?[159]

NIGHT AT THE LODGE[160]

Year's end, the Yin-Yang has shortened the daylight,
In this edge of the world, the snow has stopped, cold night.
In these small hours, the sounds of drums and horns heartbreaking,
The Milky Way over the Three Gorges, its reflections rocking
    on the water.
A thousand families wailing on the open plain, I hear the
    battles raging,
Alien tunes[161] from several directions, woodsmen and fishermen
    singing.
In the end, crouching dragons and leaping horses all go to the
    Yellow Earth,[162]
The news of human affairs no longer concerns me. Stillness.

---

[159] Sparkling wicks are commonly believed to be good omen.
[160] The poet is sojourning at Kuizhou, on the bank of the Yangzi, not far from
the Three Gorges.
[161] Literally, meaning "songs of barbarians," I.e.., of indigenous people, outside
the Middle Kingdom.
[162] The phrase "crouching dragons and leaping horses" refers to the powerful
and power-struggling men. "Yellow Earth" means the land of the dead—i.e.,
"Yellow Springs."

RETURNING TO THE DONGTUN FIELDS AFTER A BRIEF VISIT TO BAIDI

I am returning to my rice fields,
Still more work to be done before harvest.
Get ready the threshing ground, sorry for the ants,
Let village boys glean the ears from the ground.
At each pounding of the pestle, bright sunlight gleams white,
The awns gone, grains of rice shine red.
Added meals are good nourishment for old age,
The storage filled, I console myself in this drifting life.

LITTLE HANSHI[163] ABOARD BOAT

On this festive day, again I force myself to eat cold food,
Glum, I lean on the armrest, wearing a pheasant feather cap.[164]
On a spring river, I sit in a boat as though in heaven,
In my old age, the flowers look as if I see them through fog.
Juan juan, frolicking, butterflies pass by the lazy curtains,
Pian pian, weightless, gulls swoop over the rapids one by one.
Clouds white, hills green, ten thousand *li* away,
Nostalgically, I gaze straight north, to Changan.

ARRIVE AT KUIZHOU BY BOAT AND STAY OVERNIGHT ON THE SHORE

Our boat is moored overnight by the sandbank,
The pebbly shallows, the moon so lovely *juan juan*,
The wind rising, swirls the spring lamp,
The river crying, the rain streams down.

---

[163] "Hanshi" literally means day of "cold meal," which comes on the 105th day after the winter solstice. On this day, old custom forbids the use of fire; hence no cooking. "Little Hanshi" is the day after Hanshi.
[164] A cap usually worn by a recluse.

The morning bell, the misty shore drenched,
In fog is the famed Rock Hall.
Rowing the light oar, we sail away from the gulls.
Wistfully, I realize your wisdom.[165]

AT YUEYANG PAVILION

I have heard of Dongting Lake before,
Now I am up on its Yueyang Pavilion.
Wu and Chu[166] were separated by the lake, east and south.
Heaven and Earth afloat, day and night.
Not a word from my family and friends,
This old, sickly man on a lone boat.
Fighting rages on the northern mountains,
I am leaning to the railing, my tears streaming.

EVENING GLOW ON THE RIVER

North of the Chu palace in twilight,
West of the Baidi fort, a shower has passed.
The evening glow lands on the river, refracting to the rock cliff,
The lifting clouds envelop the trees, the mountain hamlet out of view.
Old age, asthma, always lying on high pillow, in this remote
     fortress village,[167]
Despondent of the time, I shut the gate early.
One shouldn't stay long where wolves and tigers roam,
In the south, this soul is still waiting to be called home.

---

[165] Is the poet addressing the gulls, thinking of their "wisdom" of living away
from the human world of turmoil? Note that Du Fu is again on the road, sailing
down the Yangzi.
[166] Two southern states during the Warring States period.
[167] Kuizhou.

DRINK IN THE STUDY, *jueju*

The moon on the lake, breeze in the wood, clear evening,
Come down from the horse, let us drink, wine is still left in the jug.
For some time I have let my sideburns grow white like a crane,
Let's not mind the neighbor's rooster announcing the daybreak.

20. WEI YINGWU (737–804?)

XIJIAN CREEK OUTSIDE CHUZHOU

Alone, I take delight in the grass growing hidden on the creek shore,
Above, yellow orioles singing in dense trees.
Spring tides, rain accompanying, come in swiftly in the evening,
No man at the ferry landing, a boat on its side.

LIFE OF SOLITUDE

Noble and lowly, though different, are the same,
All leave their homes for livelihood.
Alone, attracted by nothing of the world,
I pursue the joy of solitude.
Fine rain passes at night,
Nobody knows the spring flowers sprout out,
The blue mountains, barely daybreak,
The sparrows already chirping outside the house.
At times, I come together with holy men,
Or follow woodcutters hiking.
This simple existence just satisfies me,
Who says I despise worldly glory?

ENTERING THE HUANG HE[168] FROM GONGLUO

The blue mountains on both sides, the Luo Sui heads east,
Southeast, the valley opens for the great Huang He.
The cold trees hazy in the distant sky,
The evening light glimmers on the rippling water.

---

[168] The Yellow River.

That solitary hamlet, how many years has it been watching
    the Yi River[169]?
The sky clearing, a lone goose is coming down in the north wind.
For me tell those colleagues in Loyang,
My mind is a boat unmoored.

---

[169] A tributary of the Luo Sui.

21. SI KONGSHU (740–790?)

AT A RIVER VILLAGE

Quitting angling, I have returned, the boat left untied,
In this river village, the moon has gone down, now best to sleep.
Should a wind blow the boat away during the night,
It would only be lying in the midst of reed flowers by the shallows.

22. WANG LIE [170]

FRONTIER SONGS

(1)
Year in, year out, our bloom of youth fades away at this Altay desert,
Year after year, we lie in iron coats on these sandhills.
In this White Grass town, spring never arrives,
Over the yellow flowers on the fort, geese never cease flying.

(2)
This remote town at dusk, facing the rampart quiet,
All around, mountains rise into the blue sky over ten thousand *ren*[171].
Must I look at the bright mirror to see my hair growing white?
Sand storm coming, I know my bloom is fading.

---

[170] Dates unknown.
[171] 1 *ren* = about 7 feet.

23. HAN YU (768–824)

MOUNTAIN ROCKS

Mountain rocks strewn all over, the path barely visible,
Twilight, I arrive at the temple, bats flying.
Ascending to the hall, I sit on the steps, a light shower has passed,
Banana leaves huge, gardenias fat.
A monk, speaking of a fine Buddha painting on the old wall,
Brings a torch to illuminate it, but hardly anything to see.
Bed made, seat dusted off, soup and rice served,
The brown rice good enough to satisfy my hunger.
Night deep, I lie in peace, insects have all gone silent,
The clear moon rising from the mountain peak, shines in through
    the door.

At dawn I step out alone and wander about. No path,
In and out, up and down, roaming in the sea of mist.
The hill red, the stream green, how resplendent!
Now and then, pines and oaks ten arms' span.
Coming to a stream, I cross it barefoot, stepping on rocks,
Water rushes by, wind blows on my robe.
Such is human life to be enjoyed.
Why must one be tied to the reins, pulled by others?
Ah, two or three of my colleagues!
Why aren't they in old age still unable to retire to nature?

24. LIU ZONGYUAN (773–819)

DWELLING BY A MOUNTAIN STREAM[172]

For long I was entrapped by the official hairpins and dress cords,
By good fortune, I have been banished to this wild South.[173]
My life of leisure, in this farm neighborhood,
By chance, I am like a woodsman.
At dawn, with a plow, I turn dewy grass,
At night, with an oar, I sound the rocks in the stream.
Come and go, I meet no man,
I sing a long song to the blue sky of Chu.[174]

STROLL TO YU XI AFTER RAIN IN EARLY SUMMER

The endless rain clearing up,
I stroll around the bend of the clear creek.
Using my cane, I measure the agitated spring,
Untie my belt to circle the new bamboo growths.

---

[172] In his note, "Preface to 'The Yu Xi Poems'," Liu writes: "There is a stream north of the Guan River, which flows east into the Xiao River. . . . Because of my foolishness [yu], I violated the law and have been exiled to a place near the Xiao River. I love the stream. . . . I have named it Yu Xi [Fool's Stream]. I have bought a small hill above it and named it Yu Qiu [Fool's Hill]. If you go northeast about sixty feet from there, there is a spring, which I have also acquired and called Yu Quan [Fool's Spring]. . . . [By blocking its flow south below the hill,] I make Yu Chi [Fool's Pond] and . . . call its center Yu Dao [Fool's Island]. . . . All these places have been shamed [by these names] thanks to my foolishness [Yu]. Cited in Simosada, pp. 53, 281.

[173] Yongzhou.

[174] Chu was one of the states during the Warring States period, occupying the region south of the Yangzi in ancient China. This region is often so referred to by writers of later times.

But what is this restless feeling inside?
Stillness is what I have always sought.
By good fortune, I am here free of that hectic life of *ying ying*,
I sing a long song to cool the burning heat.

STROLL ALONE TO THE NORTH POND AT DAWN AFTER A RAINY NIGHT

The overnight clouds have lifted over the islet,
Morning sun shines on the village.
Tall trees looking down on a clear pond,
A wind surprises the night's raindrops.
My mind is at ease, free of all concerns,
Here I am at one with the present.[175]

MORNING WALK TO YU POND WITH RECLUSE XIE

After a fresh bath, I put on a light headcloth,
The morning pond, breeze and dew pure.
My mind in tune with the present, free of worldly thoughts,
All the more so in company of this man of solitude.
The haze lifts, mountains emerging in the distance,
High up in the sky, several geese fly honking.
Let the scheming mind occupy those in government,
I would rather be in tune with the spirit of Xi Huang.[176]

PASS A DESERTED VILLAGE DURING A WALK TO THE SOUTH VALLEY IN AUTUMN MORNING

Late autumn, frost and dew heavy,
After rising, I stroll down the quiet valley.

---

[175] Literally the last line reads: "At this [I] have become object-subject [*bin-zhu*]"—meaning "being free of the subject–object distinction."

[176] I.e., Fu Xi Shi. See above p. 89, n123. By the "spirit of Xi Huang," the poet is referring to the simple way of life.

Yellow leaves cover the bridge over the stream,
The deserted village, only old trees standing.
Flowers in cold air sparse, forlorn,
The quiet spring, rippling intermittently.
I have already forgotten the scheming mind,
Yet, why do I frighten the deer[177]?

OLD FISHERMAN

At night the old fisherman sleeps by the west cliff.
At dawn he scoops water from the clear Xiang River,
    burns Chu bamboo.
Haze lifts, sunrise, no man in sight,
Ai dai ai dai, only his rowing voice, the hills and waters green.
Looking back to the edge of the sky, he rows down the midstream,
Clouds over the mountain range quietly following.

SNOW ON THE RIVER

A thousand hills, birds have ceased flying,
Ten thousand paths, human tracks have vanished.
A lone boat, an old man in straw cloak and bamboo hat,
Alone fishing on the cold river in snow.

PLANT BAMBOO UNDER THE THATCHED EAVES

My roof is thatched with malaria rushes,[178]
Humid heat always invades my skin,
Frequently, serious swellings on my legs.
Humidity, how can it be good for health?

---

[177] Cf. the story of the seagulls in *Lie Zi* (see p. 73, n105).
[178] The poet is referring to the rushes from the region where he was exiled. The region was known as the land of malaria, because of the prevalence of this sickness there, which was believed to be due to its extreme humidity.

Fortunately, my east neighbor advises me,
Plant bamboo and get cool wind.
Overjoyed, it suits my wish,
Carrying a plow, I go to the foot of the west hill.
The Chu soil, full of odd-shaped rocks,
Digging it hard, I get exhausted.
Wind from the river, suddenly dusk,
Loading the bamboo in a cart, hastily I leave.
The bamboo rustles, passing Ji Pu,
Now, charmingly it stands in my quiet yard.
I hope it will take root firmly for a long life,
I will give it the tonic water from the cold spring.
At last, the night windows will not be covered,
Why would I use a feather fan?
The clean, cold air will form thick dew.
The pillow box will be cool, I already know.
The spiders will weave nets in the thick foliage,
The morning birds will nest in the high branches.
Why would this be just an escape from the bustling world?
It will also be joy to my spirit.
How delightful your tall stand, *ting ting*!
Coming from far, you promise me a quiet time.
Don't you see those creepers in the fields?
They thrive, beautiful to look at,
But truly their beauty wouldn't survive the winter cold.
How could they leave the blue mountains?

TRANSPLANTING OVER TEN CINNAMON SEEDLINGS
FROM HENGYANG TO LONGXING TEMPLE[179]

Exiled, I have come to the southern hinterland,
The clear Xiang River flows around this sacred mountain.[180]

---

[179] Longxing Temple is the place where the poet stays in the beginning of his
exile. Hengyang is about a hundred kilometers northeast of Yongzhou, where
the temple is located. Therefore the transplanting must have covered quite a
distance.
[180] Heng Shan.

Early morning, I climb the rush-covered path along the creek,
The frost has cleansed the heavy air.
Removing the overgrowth, I find hidden cinnamon plants,
Glad, their fragrant roots are small enough to be held in my hand.
They have suffered from smoke due to burning farming,
Have been cut down for firewood for ages.
When they grow by the roadside, they are not looked at,
How much more neglected in this faraway high mountain!
I will carry these cinnamon plants in a basket with their native soil,
Transplant them, so that the phoenix may visit.
The road to the temple is distant,
One rain will awaken them to flourish, nothing to learn.
The people of the south will know of their preciousness for the
     first time,
But for me, who would have discovered this?
The fine meaning cannot be conveyed,
A loyal heart is satisfying to oneself.

EARLY PLUM BLOSSOMS

Early blossoms have opened high up in the plum tree,
Shining bright far into the blue Chu sky.
The north breeze carries their night fragrance,
Heavy frost moistens their morning white.
I wish I could make a gift of the flowers to friends ten thousand
     li away,
Over the mountains and rivers.
Flowers in cold would quickly wither,
How can I console them so far away?

MEET A FARMER IN EARLY SPRING

In the southern Chu, spring comes early.
Winter cold still in the air, vegetation already in progress,
Earth's nutrients at work in bare fields,
All underground creatures compete to thrive.

Spring colors haven't arrived in this open country,
Yet the farmers are already tilling the earth.
Deep in the woods birds chirping,
Ponds and pools clear with new spring water.
Farming is truly my innate vocation,
From which captivity has kept me away all my life.
My old pond, I fear, must be buried under brushes,
The field I left behind must be full of brambles.
I longed to be in solitude, but found myself in bonds,
I dreamed of great achievements, in the end nothing came of it.
Using the old farmer's[181] words,
I express my feeling straight somewhat,
Fondly caressing my plow, I look back,
Haze stretches over the land.

FARM HOUSE, three poems

(1)
Breakfast on mat, out to work,
Driving an ox, heading to the east field.
Cocks crowing, village alleys already white,
Night light, I return from evening fields.
Zha zha, the sounds of hoes and spades,
Fei fei, crows and kites hovering over.
Devoting myself to this physical work,
I have passed one full year.
All the crops are gone to reduce my work requirement,
Out of exhaustion, I slump to sleep.
My offspring are already growing day by day,
Generation by generation repeats the same.

DRINKING WINE

This morning, feeling a little cheerless,
After rising, I open the jar of clear wine.

---

[181] By the "old farmer" the poet is referring to Tao Yuanming. Tao uses the word "caress" (*fu*) in many poems, expressing his warm feeling for a *particular* object (e.g.: a "lone pine," a "sword," and even "spring wine.")

Raising the cup, I offer libation to my ancestors,
It drives all worries from me.
Instantly my mind in another state,
Suddenly I feel the whole universe sunny.
The mountain chain loses its dark tone,
The crystalline stream turns bright and warm.
How lush the vegetation of the south gate!
How dense the trees!
Cool shades, they make their own refuge,
All evening I listen to their exquisite voices.
Get drunk? I wouldn't mind it at all,
Lie flat? There grows fragrant grass!
Those rich men of Jin and Chu,[182]
They didn't know of this way of bliss.

A LONE PINE[183]

A lone pine tree stands on a roadside in Shang Shan,
Passers-by cut it down to make the road brighter.
A thoughtful person, out of pity for the tree,
Weaves a bamboo fence, so that it would grow to the full.
Moved, I compose this poem.

A lone pine holds up its green canopy,
Its roots stretched, facing the wide road.
By endangering the passing, it puts itself in danger,
In the end, a mistake for brightness' sake.
Fortunately, it meets the goodwill of a kind man,
Cherishes the protection of this bamboo fence.
Still, its heart half alive.
It seems rain is about to come down.

---

[182] The wealth of Jin and Chu, two of the major states during the Spring–Autumn and Warring States periods (722–221 BCE), is mentioned in the *Mencius*, "Gongsun Chuo"(2).
[183] This poem has no title in the original text. Instead, it begins with the following prefatory note.

PLANT ORANGE TREES AT THE NORTH-WEST CORNER OF THE LIUZHOU CITY-WALL

I plant with my hands two hundred yellow orange trees,
Come spring, new leaves will cover the city-wall corner.
Just like Qu Yuan, I love this heavenly plant, [184]
I didn't learn from Li Heng's profiting from orange trees
    in Jingzhou. [185]
In a few years, the trees will flower, and you will hear white
    petals burst,
Who will pick the fruits and see the hanging pearls?
Should I be blessed to stay on to see the day they make a forest,
Their nutrients would also nurture this old man.

---

[184] See Qu Yuan's "In Praise of the Orange Tree" in Part 1. In his poem, Qu
Yuan calls the orange tree "God's blessed tree."
[185] During the Three Kingdoms Period (220–265), according to one record, Li
Heng, a magistrate of the state of Wu, planted for profit a thousand orange trees
in Longyang, the capital of Jingzhou. (See Simosada, 267.)

25. BAI JUYI (772–846)

TO CI EN TEMPLE

At Ci En Temple, the spring scene ends this morning,[186]
All day I have wandered, now I am leaning to the temple gate.
How sad! You cannot detain the spring from going back,
Under the purple wisteria flowers, gradually dusk sets in.

BOAT TRIP

The shadow of the sail, the sun is getting higher,
My sleep has been peaceful, I am not yet up.
Rising, I ask the oarsman.
We have already come thirty *li*.
The stove at the bow,
Cooking rice, boiling a red carp.
After eating my fill, I get up swaying,
Wash hands, rinse mouth in the autumn river.
All my life, I have dreamed of blue waves,
This morning I am sailing on this river.
Besides, I am with my family,
In the boat are my wife and children.

RAINY NIGHT ON BOAT

Over the Yangzi, the dark clouds spread slowly *you you*,
The wind blows cold *xiu xiu*.
Night rain dropping on the roof,
Night waves hit the bow.

---

[186] The full title of this poem gives the date: Third Month, Thirtieth Day. This is the last day of spring according to the Lunar Calendar.

There is a sick man on this boat,
Demoted, he is heading to Jiangzhou.

NIGHT SNOW

Already I felt the pillow and blanket cold,
Saw the window bright.
Deep night, I knew heavy snow was falling,
Just then I heard the sound of a bamboo burst.

RISE FROM A NAP AND SIT AT EASE

The nap in the backyard pavilion was fine,
I am up and sitting. Late spring afternoon.
Awaking, my vision still blurred,
No thoughts, my mind in its perfect state.
Limpid, calm, I have returned to the original oneness,
Empty, restful, free of ten thousand concerns.
Clarity itself is this state of mind,
Nothing in the world like it.
Truly the village of nothing-whatsoever,[187]
Also called the state of no-concern.[188]
Chan practice and sitting-forgetting-all,[189]
They come to the same thing.

---

[187] In the last episode of Ch. 1 of the *Zhuang Zi*, Hui Zi criticizes Zhuang Zi, by comparing the latter's idea of *wu-wei* (no-action) to a fantastically huge but useless tree. In his response Zhuang Zi says: ". . . . You have this huge tree and are worried about its uselessness. Why don't you plant this tree in the open field of the village of nothing-whatsoever (*wu he you zi xiang*), and roam around it doing nothing by its side or lie under it and sleep idly. . . ."
[188] A Buddhist notion (*bu yong chu*), referring to the state of absolute freedom from the external world.
[189] In the *Zhuang Zi* (Ch. 6), one reads an exchange between Confucius and his disciple Yan Hui, on the latter's progress in learning, at the last stage of which the pupil says: "I drop my limbs and body, let go sight and hearing, part with objects, leave behind knowledge, and become one with the great thoroughfare [i.e., Dao]. That is what I mean by "sit forgetting" (*zuo wang*).

EVENING RIVER

On the water a single streak of evening sunlight,
The river half dark blue, half red,
Lovely Third Night of Ninth Month,
The dew like pearls, the moon like a bow.

BELOW XIANGLU PEAK[190]

North of Xianglu Peak,
West of Yiai Temple,
How bright the white rocks!
The stream also flows so quietly.
Dozens of pine trees standing,
More than a thousand bamboo canes.
The pines spread their green umbrellas,
The bamboos put up their blue jade poles.
No man has lived here,
Alas, for many years!
At times monkeys and birds congregate,
All day, just wind and mist visiting, none to please.
By chance, here comes a man from the Sinking Darkness,[191]
His surname Bai, his *zi* Letian.
Usually, few things stir his interest,
Seeing this place, his mind is aroused.
As if he had found a place to end his old age,
Suddenly he forgets leaving.
Build a thatch-roofed hut, leaning it against the cliff,
Shave off the gully walls, open a tea field.

---

[190] In the original text, the poem has no title. The title provided here comes from the first phrase in the short note which precedes the poem. The note reads: "I have built a thatch-roofed hut below Xianglu Peak. I compose poems, singing what comes to my mind, and write on a stone."
[191] The poet here refers to himself by *chenmingzi*, probably suggesting one who is inept in dealing with the human world.

What to wash my ears with?
From the roof top comes down a flying spring.
What to cleanse my eyes with?
Below the steps grow white lotuses.
With a wine bottle in my left hand,
A five-stringed lute in my right hand,
In high spirits, utterly contented,
I stretch out my two legs between them.
Inspired, I sing to the sky,
In the song I say,
By nature I am a rustic,
By mistake, I was drawn into the worldly net.
When the time came, I dedicated my days to the Son of Heaven,
Now, retiring in old age, I return to the mountains.
Tired birds seek dense forests,
Thirsty fish return to clear springs.
Where would I go, abandoning this place?
So much peril and hardship in the human world.

AGAIN ON THE SAME SUBJECT[192]

(3)
The sun high, enough sleep, yet too lazy to rise,
Tiny room, double blankets, no fear of cold.
The bell of Yiai Temple, I raise my pillow,
The snow of Xianglu Peak, I roll up the bamboo screen.
Kuanglu[193] is a place where one may escape from fame,
Sima[194] a position an old official is often assigned to.
Mind at ease, body in health, that's what counts,
Must my home be found only in Changan?

---

[192] Namely, "Xianglu Peak." Four poems under this title.
[193] Another name of Xianglu Peak.
[194] Bai has been sent away from Changan to Jiangzhou with this official position,
a lighter form of exile.

A SMALL POND, two poems

(2)
A pond, something I wanted, not a big one,
About ten feet each side, yet deep and full of water.
Dew drips from lotus leaves,
Duckweeds part, you see fish swimming between.
Each time I sit facing this place,
I think of returning to a mountain stream to live.

EXILE IN JIANGNAN

I laugh at myself, a visitor from the Sinking Darkness,[195]
Formally a royal counselor,
His zeal for the country all in vain,
His misfortune incomparable.
The moment he spread his wings over the clouds,
He became a fish out of water.
The sunflower withered still turns to the sun,
The tumbleweed cut off still bids farewell to spring,[196]
This wetland, a land of despair forever,
Heaven's edge for his fading life,
How sad his miserable existence ahead,
How cold his old friendship!
The gate is grass-covered, no path.
Smoke rising no more, dust sits on the pots.
Melancholy, now he knows the holiness of wine,
Poverty, for the first time he realizes the divinity of money.

---

[195] The poet is referring to himself by *"chenmingke."* See p. 129, n191.
[196] *Chun* ("spring") is used here also as a short for a royal palace, Chun Gong ("Spring Palace").

The tiger's tail, dangerous to keep your foot on,
The sheep's entrails easily upset the wheels.[197]
Your going and staying, your success and failure,
Leave them all in the turning of the Potter's[198] wheel.

ROSES ARE OPEN, SPRING WINE RIPE[199]

In the vat is the Bamboo Leaf[200] ripe, spring brew,
By the steps the roses open, enter the summer,
Like flame, red, some light, some dark, they overwhelm the rack.
The wine feels like molasses, its green sticking to the vat base.
Let me invite you with this poem.
If you have a fanciful inclination, perhaps you can come.
Tomorrow, the morning flowers ought to be all the more beautiful,
Imagine our getting drunk together with morning drink.

SINGING VERSES ALONE IN THE MOUNTAIN

Every man has his idiosyncrasy,
Mine verse-writing.
My thousand attachments have all vanished,
This malaise alone hasn't gone yet.
Whenever I run into a fine scene,
Or when I come together with a close friend,
I recite a verse in loud voice,
Forgetting myself as if I met a spirit.

---

[197] An allusion to the following two lines in Cao Cao's poem "Hard Winter Trek": "The narrow path, winding like the sheep's entrails,/ Ruins the wagon wheels."

[198] The Creator's.

[199] The full title gives the names of the three friends to whom this poem is sent to. The last lines suggest that the poet is writing this poem as a sort of invitation. But he may be merely expressing his wish to enjoy with his friends the spring wine and the roses by the steps.

[200] The name of a famous wine.

Since becoming a man on the Yangzi,
I have lived half in the mountains.
When I have made a new poem,
I climb alone to the East Rock.
My body leaning to the white cliff,
My hands holding onto a green cinnamon tree,
I sing, startling trees and ravines,
Monkeys and birds, puzzled, all watching.
Fearing to become an object of whispering,
On purpose I seek a place where no man comes.

ENTER THE THREE GORGES AND STAY IN BADONG[201]

I don't know when we will reach our remote county,
Still I'm happy the whole family is together on this trip.
This official trip ten thousand *li*, going beyond the Three Gorges.
This life of a hundred years hangs on a single boat.
At dusk, we reach Wu Shan, rain drenching flowers,
On the Long Shui, winds often blow against the waves in
   springtime,[202]
A pair of red banners, several drum beats,
This official boat is sailing up to Badong.

ENTER QUTANG GORGE AT NIGHT

Qutang Gorge is most dangerous,
Truly perilous is night sailing!
The shores stand like a pair of screens coming together,
The sky opens like a roll of silk spreading.

---

[201] The poet is on his way to Zhongzhou County, his new place of exile. This poem and the next two are on this trip.
[202] The Long Shui is a river which flows into the Wei Shu near Changan, hence little to do with the Three Gorges. The poet is perhaps recalling the frequent spring winds on the Long Shui, which are often sung as evoking deep sadness to the traveler.

The opposite wind, huge waves raging,
In the dark a boat unhitched comes down.
Do you want to know how frightening?
It's more than Yanyudui is high.

THOUGHT AT MY FIRST VISIT TO THE GOREGES

Above, you see the mountains ten thousand *ren* high,
Below, you see the waters a thousand *zhang* down.
Dark blue between the two cliffs,
Narrow enough to let in a leaf of ship.
Qutang Gorge spews water straight out,
Yanyudui rises high in the middle straight up.
Not yet night, yet the black rocks dark,
No wind, yet rising waves white.
Large rocks stand like swords,
Small rocks like animal teeth.
Not a single step allowed,
But a thousand, three hundred *li* to go.

How slender the rope pulling the boat,
How unsteady the boatman's feet!
One false move, the whole ship be gone,
My life tied to this.
One is always told, Be loyal and truthful,
And you may live even among the savages.
Since time immemorial, drowned here were all non-*cunzi?*[203]
Well, with my fate, in my time?
I have been out of step with the world, the saying is hard to count on.
Always I worry, this man of no talent
Will one day die nameless.

---

[203] Meaning "non-noblemen" or "men of low moral character." *Cunzi* means
"son of a prince" or "man of high moral character."

WINTER SUN ON THE BACK

What a bright winter sunrise!
The sun shines in this corner of my house.
My back warm, I sit with my eyes closed,
Balmy sensation comes to my skin.
At first, like drinking fine wine,
Or as if awaking from hibernation.
Body mellow, all my bones relaxed,
Mind at ease, free of all thoughts.
Boundless, I forget where I am,
My mind is one with the void.

SPRING RIVER

Hot and cold, dusk and dawn, in quick transition,
Unawares, already two years in Zhongzhou.
The office gate closed, I hear only the pounding of the drum,
　　morning and evening,
Climbing to the upper floor, I just watch the ships going
　　and coming.
The orioles chirping tempt me down to the flowers below,
Detained by the colors of the grass, I sit by the shore.
Only the spring river a view hard to be tired of,
Water traveling quietly around the sand, between pebbles.

STROLL ON THE EAST HILL

In the morning I go up the East Hill and stroll,
In the evening I go up the East Hill and stroll.
What do I love about the East Hill?
I love its new trees growing.
I planted them in the beginning of the year,
They were flourishing by the late spring.
I planted them haphazardly, following my impulse,
Not in rows. I don't know how many.

The shades of the trees shift with the slanting sunlight,
Fragrant air drifts in faint breeze.
Birds alight on the new leaves,
Butterflies fly away from the shriveled flowers.
Quietly carrying my cane of spotted bamboo,
I walk slowly, dragging my sandals of yellow hemp.
Want to know how often I go up and down there?
The green swath of weeds has turned a white path.

SAIL ALONG THE WIND

In this mountain town, though desolate,
There bamboos and trees grow splendidly.
The salary from the county is certainly not great,
Yet sufficient to feed and clothe my family.
External troubles come from the mind,
With the mind at ease, troubles cease by themselves.
I still try to forget my home.
Who can calculate the government employment?
The mind contented, far and near are equal,
Accepting what comes your way, you go north and south.
Returning home is surely desirable,
Yet you may find it also satisfying to live at the edge of the sky.

FAREWELL TO THE FLOWERS AND TREES OF THE EAST HILL
I PLANTED, two *jueju*

(1)
Having sojourned for two years in this river town,
I have grown attached to all the grass, trees, birds, and fish.
Where in this place would I not again and again turn around with
    tender feelings?
The peach and apricot trees I planted have grown big.

---

[204] An allusion to a song in the *Shi Jing*, "Wild Pear Tree," in which the people
sing the good rule of the Lord of Shao, who camped under a wild pear tree.

(2)
Flowers and trees, stay well, don't languish,
When spring comes, be as in springs gone by.
Next year, a new magistrate will occupy the residence,
It won't hurt you that he be also a lover of flowers.

TO THE SPRING LAKE

Spring comes to this lake, like a picture.
The mountain peaks swarming around, the water spreading calm,
The pine rows on the mountain breasts, in a thousand shades of green,
The moon dots a grain of pearl in the middle of the lake.
Green wool tips, out of the rice seedlings,
Blue silk ribbons, out of the cattail.
I cannot give up Hangzhou to leave,
It's this lake that half retains me.

ON POETRY

New poems, day in, day out, I compose,
Not that I love fame.
Old poems, from time to time, I change,
Poetry greatly appeals to my born nature.
Should I remain forever magistrate of this county,
I wouldn't seek return to the capital.
I only wish to be by the lakes and rivers,
Spend my life, reciting poems.

FAREWELL TO THE COUNTY FOLK

The elders block my departure,
Wine jars fill this farewell table.
Not a single wild pear tree,[204] {note opposite}
Why are tears in your eyes?
Taxes heavy, poor houses many,

Farmers hungry, too many rice paddies go dry.
I have only made a reservoir of lake,[205]
May it save you from drought!

EARLY AUTUMN ON THE POND

Lotuses and water chestnuts, the green leaves all mingled,
Early autumn, the pond full.
Already cool air by the north railing,
Late sunlight shines low, the east bamboo hedge.
Cicadas, satiated with dew, sing languidly,
Willow trees, dry from wind, have lost their vigor.
I am past Pan Yue[206] by twenty years,
Why must I be more melancholic?

A CLEAR VIEW FROM THE RIVER PAVILION

The wind turning away, the clouds gather,
The mist lifting, the water surface opens.
A rainbow in the clear sky, the bridge emerging,
An autumn goose, the boatman singing.
This county in peace, I am no longer in office.
My home far away, no reply yet,
Tomorrow morning the Double Ninth,
Who will offer me a chrysanthemum cup?

LATE SPRING, twenty poems[207]

(9)
Late spring, where is it so lovely?
Spring advances at the home of this banished man.

---

[205] Bai Juyi had built a reservoir of the West Lake of Hangzhou, while in office
as magistrate of the county,
[206] A poet of Western Jin (265–304), who lamented the appearance of white
hair at age 32 in his poem.
[207] Bai Juyi composes these poems, rhyming with "Late Spring, twenty poems"
by his friend, Yuan Zhen.

A cup of wine on the Day of Hanshi,[208]
Ten thousand *li* away, the flowers in my old garden.
Here, the malaria heat[209] steamy like fire.
Time flies like a chariot.
Worrying about an owl's arrival,
I fear only the sun slanting.[210]

(12)
Late spring, where is it so lovely?
Spring advances at a fisherman's home.
The pine inlet, the moon follows his oar in the water.
The peach shore, the flowers fall on the boat.
He throws baits in, moves the boat,
Turning the reel, he pulls the line.
Breeze through the marsh, *xiao xiao*,
Wind blowing, the line slanting.

TWO OCCASIONAL POEMS

(2)
With sunrise I get up, wash myself and comb hair,
After dusting off my clothes, enter the meditation room.
Stillness, no thoughts,
I just watch the incense burning in front.
Only when the sun is high up, I take a meal,
Light, neither meat nor refined rice.
Fine or coarse, I take whatever is available,
It satisfies me, filling my belly.
At noon I take off my cap and hairpin,
Rest on the bed by the window.

---

[208] For "Hanshi" see p. 111, n163.
[209] See p. 121, n178.
[210] The last two lines are allusion to a story of Gu Yi (200–168 BCE), who, during his exile in Changsha, saw an owl fly into his room one evening and took it as an ominous sign.

Cool breeze arriving,
In bed, I reach the blissful state of Fu Xi.[211]
The sun in the west, I drag my cane and sandals,
Strolling in the forest and by the pond,
Or drink a cup of tea,
Or chant a stanza from a poem.
After sundown, I often skip the meal,
At times, only asking for wine.
How do I spend evening hours leisurely?
The music of "Rainbow Dress"[212] on the autumn evening.
Divide a day in five periods,
Usually I follow a constant schedule of activities and rests.
I enjoy health in old age,
Don't mind being busy in midst of leisure.
Right and wrong are strung on the same thread,
The world and I in union, both forgotten.
If asked what this state is,
This is the village of nothing-whatsoever.[213]

BY THE POND

Niao niao, the cool wind blowing,
Qi qi, the cold dew dripping.
The orchid has withered, its flowers begin to turn white,
The lotus shriveled, its leaves still blue.
Alone standing is the crane that nests in the sandbank,
In pairs fly the fireflies, lighting over the water.
What would I do in this desolate scene?
Besides, I am waking from wine.

[211] See p. 89, n123.
[212] A dance music played at the court of Emperor Xuangzong of the Tang.
[213] See p. 128, n187.

THE WEST POND OF THE PREFACTURE BUILDING

The willow trees listless, the bough tips moving.
Ripples on the pond, the ice has opened.
Today no one knows whose scheme this is,
Spring wind, spring water, has arrived all at once.

SONGS SUNG AT MOMENTS OF *XING*,[214] five poems,
with prefatory note

Seventh Year of Dahe, Fourth Month, I resigned from the office of
governor of Henan, and returned to my house in Ludaoli. A modest
house, self-sufficient in provisions. Nothing in need, nothing to work
for. Sometimes singing, sometime dancing. Life at ease, carefree. One
may say I am one happy man between the Huang He and the Luo Shui.[215]
Whenever my spirit is so moved, I recite a poem. I now have five poems,
each titled by its first line.

(3) A Little Boat in the Pond
I keep a little boat in the pond,
In the boat a small folding table,
Before the table a jug of newly brewed wine.
Alone I drink it, alone I savor it.
Its fragrance like the spring day air,
Its radiance like the autumn river light.
You may cleanse your scheming mind,
You may wash your soiled entrails.[216]

---

[214] The two-character compound word *yong xing* in the title is hard to translate.
Literally it means "to sing *xing*." By "moments of *xing*" I mean "moments when
the spirit is moved or aroused." The English word "inspired" may seem close to
xing in this sense. But "inspiration" connotes its *external* origin (e.g., "inspired"
by God or Holy Spirit). But this connotation of external source is absent in
"moments of *xing*." Thus *yong xing* means a poem or song one composes as one's
own spirit is so *moved*.
[215] The two rivers which flow north and south of Loyang.
[216] The entrails were believed to be the organ of feelings.

The shores bending, the sailing slow,
One bend, one cup.
I have no idea how many bends make me drunk,
Once drunk, I enter the realm of nothing whatsoever.
Around and around, between the pond islands,
The bamboo by the water dark blue.
Body in peace, nothing in mind,
The day is long for me to enjoy.
Had I not forgotten the world,
My mind, though in peace, would be busy.
Hadn't the world forgotten me,
I would find it hard to hide, though in retirement,
I am now different,
My self and the world have forgotten each other.

(4) Fourth Month, the Pond Full
Fourth Month, the pond full,
The turtles swim, the fish leap out.
I also love my pond,
By the pond, I put up a hut.
Humans and fish, though different species,
Their joys come to the same.
For now I'll be your companion,
Roaming, we will spend days together.
Don't miss the blue sea,
Be at home among the rushes.
I'll forget the blue clouds,[217]
Single-bar gate, thatched roof, sufficient to cover my knees.
After all, I am now with you fellows,
By nature, I'm not of a dragon species,
Even if clouds bring rain,
That would only be a pond affair.

---

[217] "Blue clouds" (*qing yun*) means "youthful dreams" such as high office.

26. DU MU (803–852)

SPRING IN THE SOUTH OF THE YANGZI, *jueju*

A thousand *li*, orioles singing, green shining on red.
Riverside villages, mountain hamlets, wine shop flags in the wind.
The four hundred eighty temples of the Southern dynasties,
How many of the halls and terraces in this misty rain?

MOUNTAIN TRIP

High up in the cold mountain, the rocky path goes sideways,
A house is standing where white clouds rise.
Stopping the carriage, rapt, I admire the maple forest in the evening,
Frost-bitten leaves redder than flowers of Second Month.[218]

HIKING TO QI SHAN ON NINTH DAY

The autumn scenes float on the river, the early geese flying over,
With a friend, I climb the verdant mountain breast, carrying a
    wine bottle.
In the world of dust you rarely meet hearty laughter,
We must return wearing chrysanthemums all over our heads.
Celebrate this fine holiday only with drink,
No use lamenting the sinking sun from the terrace.
The old goes, the new comes, just like this,
Must one ascend Niu Shan to wet the robes with tears?[219]

---

[218] By the lunar calendar, i.e., early spring.
[219] During the Spring–Autumn period, the Duke of Qi is said to have climbed
Niu Shan and lamented death, which would separate him from his domain
below.

27. WEN TINGYUN (812?–870?)

CLIMBING SHANG SHAN EARLY

I rise early, the carriage bell ringing,
This traveler on the road, nostalgic for his home village.
The cock crowing, the moon is over the thatched inn,
Human tracks on the frost-covered wood bridge.
Oak leaves have fallen on the mountain path,
Orange flowers bright by the walls of the post.
It reminds me of my dream at Duling,
The curving dike full of ducks and geese.

28. MEI YAOCHEN (1002–1060)

HIKE TO LU SHAN

Appealing to my yearning for the wild,
A thousand hills rise high and low.
Magnificent peaks shift as I climb,
Walking alone on a dark trail, I get lost.
Frost comes down, bears climb up the trees,
The forest desolate, deer drinking at the stream.
A house anywhere?
A rooster crows beyond the clouds.

29. OUYANG XIU (1007–1072)

PLAYFUL REPLY TO YUAN ZHEN

Spring wind, I wonder if it ever visits this edge of the sky,
Second Month, yet nothing blooms in this mountain town.
The late snow weighs on branches, oranges still hanging,
The freezing thunder frightens bamboo shoots out of the ground.
At night, hearing the returning geese, I think of home wistfully,
Sick in bed on New Year's Day, I have been keen to nature's scenes.
Once in Loyang, I sat in the middle of flowers in a garden,
Blooming late in this countryside, but nothing to lament.

PRACTICING CALLIGRAPHY

Practicing calligraphy, I was unaware of nightfall coming,
Only puzzled by the west window darkening.
The eyes already impaired, my vision blurring,
Unable to distinguish between the thick and thin of the ink.
In life people fail to realize what they do,
Labor hard, yet never regret it.
They get empty names,
Glory is momentary, it quickly goes away.
Would calligraphy practice alone be such?
Keeping this in mind, I shall take it as a lesson.

30. WANG ANSHI (1021–1086)

APRICOT FLOWERS ON THE NORTH DIKE

Spring water all around the dike, apricot flowers are open,
Bewitchingly, they dominate this spring scene.
Even if blown away by spring wind to become snow,
Far better than being crushed in dirt on the south road.

IN EARLY SUMMER

A stone bridge, a thatched house, by the bend of the shores,
Water flows rapidly between the two dikes.
Sunny day, the breeze carries wheat mist,
The time when the grass hidden in green shades excels flowers.

AT ZHONG SHAN

Silently, the creek flows around the bamboo grove,
West of the bamboo, flowers delight in gentle spring air.
Under the thatched eaves I sit all day, enjoying the view,
Not a single bird's sound, the mountain looming ever stiller.

ON THE YANGZI

North of the Yangzi, the grey autumn sky half open,
The rain clouds in the morning sky drift low.
The blue mountains surrounding, where does the water go?
Suddenly, there come a thousand sails, appearing, disappearing.

31. SU SHI (1036–1101)

MOUNTAIN VIEW FROM THE RIVER

From the ship the mountains look like racing horses,
Quickly pass several hundreds of them in pack.
The front ones, sharp peaks, suddenly change their shapes,
The rear ones, in congestion, flee as if frightened.
Looking up, I see a little path winding around the slope,
High up a traveler barely visible.
From the ship, I raise my hand, wanting to speak to him.
The lone boat sails away like a flying bird.

RHYMING WITH ZIYOU'S "TREADING THE GREEN"[220]

Spring wind rouses light dust on the roads,
For fun-seekers the first day to enjoy the arrival of spring.
Away from work, people find roadside drinking fun,
Wheat short, not yet fearful of carriage wheels.
City-dwellers, tired of city-walls,
Make commotion at dawn, leaving the city empty.
Songs and drums surprise hills, shaking all vegetation,
Picnic baskets strewn over the field, crows and kites approach
    as if tamed.
Who is that man drawing a crowd, calling himself a priest?
Blocking the road, he sells good-fortune tickets, his look fierce.
Good for silkworms, your cocoons will get as big as jars,
Good for livestock, your sheep will get as big as deer!
Passers-by do not necessarily believe these words,
But reluctantly buy the tickets as evil-chasers for the new spring.

---

[220] Ziyou is Su Shi's younger brother, also a poet. The two brothers wrote
numerous poems to each other, often rhyming with the other's verses.

The priest, grabbing money, straightaway goes to a wine shop,
Dead drunk he declares, my tickets work magic.

DAQIN TEMPLE

Far in the flood of sunlight ends this quiet river plain,
The mountain hem green, undulating.
Suddenly I see a lone pagoda in the distance,
Alone bright against the surrounding mountains.
Trusting my feet, I have come far, seeking solitude.
At a gust of wind, I stand back, surprised, and look.
Fields and paddies spread like sea,
All inclining to the east, endless.

A VIEW OF HUAI SHAN AFTER YINGKOU,
ON THIS DAY I ARRIVE AT SHOUZHOU

I am heading to the Yangzi and the East Sea, sailing day and night,
Maple leaves, reed flowers, the joy of autumn endless.
The flat expanse of the Huai river suddenly confuses near and far
    in the sky,
For a long time the green hills rise and fall with the boat.
Shouzhou, I already see its White Stone Pagoda,
Still our short oars fail to go around the Brown Reed Hill.
Waves calm, wind mild, I look ahead in vain,
My friends are long waiting in the bluish mist.

VISIT TO JINSHAN TEMPLE

My home is where the Yangzi originates,
My official career has sent me straight down to where the river
    enters the sea.
They say the swirl reaches ten feet high,
The weather cold, the trace of water visible on the sand.

A *chan* stone on the south shore of Zhongling Spring,
From of old it appears, disappears with the waves.
I climb to the hilltop to have a view toward my home region,
South of the river, north of the river, green mountains one
     after another.

Nostalgic. Fearing the night coming, I inquire about a return boat,
The mountain monk insists on keeping me for a sunset view.
The breeze makes exquisite patterns on the vast river surface,
Ragged clouds over the half sky, as red as the tails of overstrained
     fish.[221]
At this moment, over the river appears the early moon,
     its ring around,
In the second night watch, the moon goes down, the sky in utter
     darkness.

The middle of the river bright as if lighted by torches,
Flying flames illuminate mountains, frightening roosting crows.
Flustered, I go back to bed, mystified,
Neither ghost nor human, what was it after all?

Rivers and mountains are like this, yet I don't return to my
     mountains,
The spirit of the Yangzi displays a wonder to shock my fixation.
I beg for the spirit's forgiveness. Why not quit all?
Had I a field, would I not return, like rivers?

NEW YEAR'S EVE, ON DUTY AT THE PREFECTURE OFFICE[222]

New Year's Eve, I should go home early.
Office work detains me,
Holding the brush, I cry at my work.

---

[221] Apparently, it was believed that a fish would get its tail red when over-
strained.
[222] The full title reads: "On New Year's Eve, on duty at the prefecture office,
and the jail full. In the evening I cannot go to my residence. Thereupon, I
compose a poem on the wall."

Pity these inmates bound in the jail,
The simple folks, doing things for their livelihood,
Fall into the net, without knowing the shame.
I, too, covetous of a meager salary,
Following the same old track, have lost a chance to retire.
No point discussing which is wise and which foolish,
Equally, a scheme to eat.
Who could give them a brief leave?
Losing words out of pity, I am ashamed before the ancient sages.

DRUNK AT WANGHULOU PAVILION, five *jueju*

(1)
The dark clouds spill black ink, yet fail to cover the mountains,
The white rain sprinkles pearls, invading the ship.
The gusty wind passes, suddenly blowing everything away,
Below Wanghulou the water is blue like the sky.

(2)
The fish and turtles, released in the water, come to people, following,
The lotus flowers, master-less, open everywhere.
Pillow over the water, let the mountains rise and fall,
The boat in wind roams with the moon.

ON THE WAY TO XINCHENG, two poems

(1)
The east wind, knowing my desire to go on a hike,
Blows away from the eaves the sound of endless rain.
Bright clouds, as if downy caps, over the mountain peaks,
Early sun a brass gong hanging from the treetops.
The wild peach flowers smile over the low bamboo hedges,
Willow branches swaying by the stream, the crystalline water
    flows on sand.
The farm houses on the west hill, this should be their happiest time,
Boil cress, roast bamboo shoots, lunch to be delivered to the field.

VISIT TO ZUTAYUAN TEMPLE DURING ILLNESS

Purple plums, yellow melons, the village fragrant,
Black cap, white hemp robe, the monk's habit cool.
This country temple, the gate closed, the pine shadows shifting.
Pillow sideways by the breezy window, this visitor dreams long.
I've got this peace thanks to my illness, not bad at all,
Resting your mind is the best medicine, no better formula.
The monk, generous with the spring water by the steps,
Gives me a ladle and a barrel and lets me use it as much as I please.

ON THE WALL OF NORTH TERRACE AFTER SNOW, two poems

(1)
Dusk. Fine rain still comes down *xian xian*,
The night quiet, no wind, the air is getting colder.
I feel my bedclothes damp, as if water sprayed on,
Unaware of a mound of salt already piling in the yard.
Daybreak. Sunlight comes to my study curtain,
Half-moon, cold sound, snow falling from the painted eaves.
Out of curiosity, I get the North Terrace swept to see Ma'er Shan,
Its two peaks, not yet buried, point into the sky.

REPLY TO ZHONGBODA OF LULIANG [223]

A swarming throng of mountains surround the city of Suzhou,
Your official lodging is located in the remote village of Xianshui.
The villagers, indigent, share their life with the deer,
The market, ill-provided, no chickens or pigs.

The Yellow River was coming to the village from west, you weren't
   aware,
You merely wondered if the Si River was rushing by.

---

[223] Zhongboda was a local official in Luliang, outside the city of Suzhou, of which Su Sh was governor at the time of the huge flooding of the Yellow River (1077), which this poem refers to.

At night, you heard the beating of earthen casks on the shores,
In the morning, you discovered the albatrosses floating on the
  white waves.
Luliang, the very throat of the Yellow River since ancient times,
Its ten thousand acres of land, how was it flooded over in a single lap?
You watched the water enter the village, sweeping the houses away.
The villagers and officials all ran away, leaving you behind,
At a loss, all roads cut off, where would you go?
You composed a poem of your house broken, a grounded kite
  lamenting.

The weather getting cold, frost heavy, the water receded,
You only saw the trace of sand remaining on the roof tiles.
You came to Suzhou, we sat together, all seemed like a nightmare.
I too had barely escaped becoming a fish or turtle.
Soon entertainers were brought in to cheer us up.
Wildly, we drank, emptying our wine barrel.

Thinking of how cold your lodging,
I send you a new poem and wine to warm you up a little.
Life is like a brief sojourn, why not enjoy it?
Let the red candles burn the dusk.
The levees are not yet built, the Huai and Si Rivers are full,
The old river courses have disappeared, all the damages still
  remaining.
Next year's work will surely be immense.
I should be carrying dirt baskets on my shoulders ahead of the
  prisoners.
A thousand workers will be allotted to quarrying rocks,
A thousand sledgehammers thundering at the blue mountain foot.
High walls will rise like iron, the rapids will flow fast.
Laughing, we shall turn away the swelling water and watch it
  rush by.
The farmers will swing their elbows, no longer trembling,
The autumn crops will cover the fields, like clouds.
Again, we should celebrate this, drinking.
For you, the drums will be beaten, the golden jugs go around.

AWAKE AT NIGHT ON A BOAT

A breeze blows *xiao xiao*, over water-oats and cattails,
I open the hatch to see rain, but moonlight floods the lake.
Boatmen and water birds both dream the same dream,
Frightened, a large fish leaps like a fleeing fox.
The night late, man and creature unconcerned with each other,
My shadow and I alone awake, at play.
Dark tides wash over the shore, I mourn the earthworms freezing,
The setting moon hanging from a willow tree, I see a spider hanging.
My life rushes ahead in the midst of agonies,
Clear, unsullied scenes passing by my eyes, can't they tarry
    for a moment?
Cocks crowing, bells ringing, a hundred birds scattering,
At the bow the drums beat, shouts fly back and forth.

FOUR TREES AT YUSHITAI. four poems[224]

(3) Bamboo
Today the south wind arriving
Blows into confusion the bamboo in the yard.
The noise, high and low, rhythmic,
As if armor and weapons in wild contact.
Wind or snow, how severe,
It may break but cannot disgrace the bamboo,
Once snow lifted, the bamboo quickly recovers,
Scattering its green jade magnificently.
How is my old mountain home?
Autumn rain may ruin the chrysanthemums by the bamboo hedge.
I wish I knew the health of the bamboo,
When I return, I will sweep the green of the south side.

---

[224] Poems written during Su's incarceration at Yushitai.

ON TWENTY-EIGHTH DAY OF TWELFTH MONTH, I RECEIVE
A PARDON WITH APPOINTMENT TO THE ENGINEERING
OFFICE OF HUANGZHOU, two poems

(1)
I have finished my incarceration of a hundred days, it's as if spring
    has arrived,
How to enjoy my remaining years, my utmost concern.
Outside the gate, I walk around, feeling the breeze on my face,
Our galloping horses race one after another, magpies make a racket.
Back home I face my wine cup, all has been like a dream,
I pick the brush to try a poem, I feel already inspired.
Why must I dig deep to fix the blame for this incident?
I have thieved my emolument in the past, any other cause is there?

(2)
All my life writing has brought me into trouble,
Quit this. I don't mind my fame falling.
Even if the frontier horse should return later,[225]
I wouldn't join the boys' cockfight at court.[226]
Tao Yuanming, quitting his job at Pengze, was so poor that he had
    no wine,
Vimalakirti[227] was sick, leaning to his table, but had his wife.
Something that makes me smile,
Ziyou dispatched an urgent petition on my behalf and was sent
    to Jiangxi.[228]

---

[225] This line refers to a story in *Huainan Zi*, whose moral is that one never knows
what brings good or bad fortune. According to the story, an old frontier man
loses his horse, which, however, returns later with another horse, one of a famous
breed, from the northern steppes.
[226] Here Su is alluding to an episode in a Tang romance, which tells of a boy
whom Emperor Ming Huang brings to his court and puts him in charge of cock-
fight. By "boy's cockfight" Su is referring to "fight" for government office.
[227] A lay disciple of the Buddha.
[228] Su adds the following note to the poem: "Ziyou, learning of my incarceration,
appealed for atonement of my sin through his own demotion. . . ." As a conse-
quence, Ziyou, Su's brother, was sent from Suiyang to Yunzhou.

PLUM BLOSSOMS, two poems

(1)
Spring has arrived, the stream runs down a dark ravine, murmuring,
Bright are white plum blossoms in the midst of vegetation.
All night, an easterly wind blows, splitting rocks,
In company of the flying snow flurries[229] off and on, I cross the mountain pass.

(2)
Would anyone come to this dark ravine with wine to admire them?[230]
They bloom by themselves, stay languid, and in the end fall in sorrow.
Fortunately, this clear stream makes its course with three hundred bends,
I don't mind the flowers accompanying me down to Huangzhou.[231]

EAST SLOPE, [232] eight poems
with a prefatory note

For two years since my arrival here in Huangzhou, my hardship from poverty has increased day by day. My friend, Ma Zhengqing, sorry to see my not having enough to eat, requested from the county several dozen *mu* of land, a former army camp site, and had me cultivate it for my own use. The land had long been left wild and had turned into a field of brambles, tile pieces, and rocks. Besides, this year we have been having severe drought. The work of tilling has nearly exhausted my muscle strength. Sighing, I drop the plow and write these poems to console myself for my hard labor. I hope that the coming years' harvest will make me forget this hardship.

---

[229] I.e.., plum flowers.
[230] Refers to "white plum blossoms" in the first poem.
[231] Su Shi's destination of exile.
[232] The title "East Slope" (Dong-Po) refers to the field he cultivates. Su's literary name comes from this title. As a poet, he is better known as "Su Dongpo."

(1)

No man looks after an abandoned earthwork,
The decayed fences covered by sagebrushes.
Who could give his muscle strength for nothing?
No return for labor at the end of year.
Here comes a solitary traveler,
Whom heaven has driven into this corner, from which
    not to escape.
Quietly I come and pick up tile pieces and rocks,
A year of drought, the soil is lean.
From the middle of brambles and weeds hard to
    walk through,
I am trying to produce an inch of edible plants.
Sighing deeply, I let go of my plow,
When will my food closet rise?

(2)

Wild fields grow beyond control,
But high and low terrains have each their use.
Plant rice in damp lowland,
Jujubes and chestnuts on the eastern hillside.
A man from Shu, living south of the river,
Has already agreed to give me mulberry seeds.
Fine bamboo is not hard to grow,
But I fear its roots spread all over.
In the meantime, I will select a fine lot
To build my house according to my plan.
The servant boy, who has been burning dry grass,
Runs in to report his discovery of a hidden well.
A single full meal not yet to be expected,
But a gourdful of water now secured.

(3)

Since old times a little stream has come down the hill,
Originating from the mountain pass way up.
Flowing through city-walls and passing villages,
Polluted, it nourishes tumbleweeds.
In the end it becomes the Ke Clan pond,

Ten *mu*,[233] where fish and crayfish congregate.
Due to drought this year, the stream has also dried up,
Dead duckweeds plastered on its cracked dirt bottom.
Last night clouds appeared over the south mountain,
Rain came, saturating the ground more than plowshare deep.
Water ran through the old ditches,
Knowing my clearing of weeds and brambles.
Old cress roots in mud,
An inch long, ah, they have survived.
When will they issue their white buds?
Spring pigeons, perhaps a dish of mixed salad.[234]

(4)
I plant rice before the Qingming Festival,[235]
I can enumerate joyful things to come.
Fine rain darkens the spring pond,
Rice shoots stick out of water like needles, you hear happy words.
Rice seedlings divided, early summer arrives,
Joy grows as wind raises the leaves.
The moon bright, you see dewdrops forming,
Each a pearl on a line hanging.
Autumn comes, ears frosted grow heavy,
Falling upside down, propping up one another.
But you hear from between ridges
The noise of locusts flying as if showers.
Fresh out of a mortar, rice goes into the steamer,
Grains of jade brighten the bamboo basket.
I have for long eaten rice from government storage,
Reddish and putrid, no better than mud cake.
From now on, I should appreciate this new taste,
I have already promised my mouth and belly.

---

[233] Approx. 16 acres.
[234] Attached to this poem is the following note: "People of Shu value salad of celery buds as a delicacy. They prepare it, mixing it with pigeon meat." Su comes from Shu, today's Sichuan region.
[235] The 15th day after the vernal equinox.

(5)

A good farmer spares soil energy,
How fortunate! The ground has been fallow these ten years.
Mulberry trees still far from maturity,
Only wheat may be counted on.
Though less than a month since planting,
It already covers the earth, all green.
An old farmer tells me,
Don't let seedlings grow too many leaves.
If you want plenty of flour for steaming,
You must let cows and sheep graze in the field.
I bow to him repeatedly for his kind advice,
When my belly is full, I will not forget his words.

RAIN ON THE DAY OF HANSHI, two poems

(1)

Since my arrival in Huangzhou
Hanshi has come and gone three times.
Every year I wish to enjoy springtime,
But it passes without allowing me to do so.
This year too, wretched rain,
The two months have been woeful, autumn weather.
In bed I hear rain falling on *haitang*[236] flowers,
Their red and white petals getting soiled in mud.
During the middle of night, a man of extraordinary strength
Stealthily carries the spring away.[237]
Would that sick boy be different
Who gets up from his sickbed, finds his head white?

---

[236] *Rosa rugosa*, which produces red or white flowers.
[237] Refers to a passage in *Zhuang Zi* (Ch. 6), where Zhuang Zi uses the figure of
a man of extraordinary strength who in the middle of night carries away a boat
hidden in a ravine and a mountain hidden in a marsh.

(2)

The spring river tries to come in the door,
The rain pouring harder, never ending.
My hut is like a fishing boat
Under the rain clouds dark *meng meng*,
Empty kitchen, dried vegetables cooking,
Broken stove, wet rushes burning.
How do you know today is Hanshi?
Just look at the crows, the paper money[238] in their beaks.
The royal palace deep inside nine gates,
My family cemetery ten thousand *li* away.
Truly, I wish to lament my dead end,
Dead ashes, however hard you may blow, won't rise.

STAYING OVERNIGHT IN THE MOUNTAIN ON THE WAY TO THE SHITIAN POST

Along the stream, the green mountains, over three hundred ridges,
I climb up in one stretch, riding a fleet horse in summer shirt.
On a mountain slope a house stands in a tall bamboo grove,
A clear spring alongside the path knows my thirst.
Grass sandals soft, bamboo cane light,
Straw mat smooth, pine bed also fragrant.
Deep night, wind and dew fill the inner yard,
I see only a lone firefly flickering in the air.

ON THE WALL OF XILIN TEMPLE

Seen from the side, a mountain range, from the front, a peak.
Seen from far, near, high, and low, never the same.
You don't know the true face of Lu Shan,
Only because you are in the mountain.

---

[238] On Hanshi, it was customary to burn paper money at the grave cites.

SUNSHENLAO SENDS ME AN INK-STONE, four poems

(4)

My trouble originates from offense by poetry,[239]
For long my friends have warned me.
Five years, living in this river town,
I have shut my mouth, washing off my remaining debt.
Recently, I have done writing again little by little,
The pleasure from this scribbling is like scratching an itch.
Sir, you don't warn me,
Instead, you send me a pillory of poetry,[240]
The dark sheen of the ink evokes a fanciful imagination,
Its dots and strokes give wondrous impressions.
A poem done, I laugh,
My old disease must have met shrimps or crabs.[241]

MIRAGE AT SEA, with a prefatory note

I had heard of the mirage at Dengzhou for a long time. A local elder told
me, "It usually comes in spring or summer. Now it's late in the year. It
can't be seen." After arriving here to take up my post, I was to leave in
five days. I would hate to miss the mirage. So I prayed at the shrine of
Guangde Wang, the Sea God. On the following day, the mirage
appeared, so I wrote this poem.

To the east spread clouds and sea, limitless void,
A host of immortals appear and disappear in hollow brightness.

---

[239] See p. 154, n224. Su Shi was incarcerated at Yushitai because of his poem,
which was taken as a criticism of a certain policy of the court.
[240] The two-character word, *shi xie*, literally means "instrument of poetry." Here
the poet is using the word in a double sense: namely, the ink-stone first as an
instrument of writing, and second, as something that may lead to his trouble
with the government because of the writing. The character *xie* alone can mean
an instrument of punishment.
[241] Crabs and shrimps were believed to cause the hives. In this line, the poet is
ironically suggesting that his old habit (itch?) of writing poetry is coming back
thanks to the gift of the ink-stone.

The undulation of the floating world generates the ten thousand
    forms,
How could there be a palace of pearls hidden behind shell gates?

My mind knows that all visible things are illusory,
But to satisfy my eyes and ears, I plead with the god for his work.
The season is cold, water icy, heaven and earth closed,
But for me please arouse the dragons from hibernation and whip them
    into action.
Many-storied pavilions and green hills emerge from the frosty dawn,
A wonder to surprise centenarians.

What a man gets you may gain by force,
Outside the human world not a thing to be taken by force, who could
    lord it over?
I made my request insolently, which was not denied,
Truly, mine has been man-made misfortune, no hardship from
    heaven.

When the governor of Chaoyang[242] was returning from exile in
    the south,
He was overjoyed to see the soaring peaks of Heng Shan.
He said to himself, My honesty has moved the mountain spirit.
Rather, didn't he know that the Creator had pity on his feeble figure?
I laugh, how would such a thing come by easily?
The god's gift to you[243] was indeed generous.

Slanting sunlight over ten thousand *li*, a lone bird vanishes,
I see only the emerald sea, green bronze finely polished.
This new poem, flowery words, what good is it?
It too will turn into nothing, fading away with the east wind.

---

[242] Han Yu.
[243] Gift to the poet himself?

TO LIU JINGWEN[244]

Gone are the lotus leaves, no umbrella to put up in rain,
The chrysanthemum still in bloom, its branches contemptuous
   of frost.
A fine scene of the year, you ought to remember,
Above all, this is the season when the citron is yellow,
   the orange green.

FAREWELL TO ZIYOU[245] IN RAIN

Paulownia tree at the yard rim,
In three years, I have seen you three times.[246]
Two years ago, on my way to Yingzhou,
I saw you weep in autumn rain.
Last year, again, in autumn rain
On my return from Yangzhou.
This year, I am on my way to Dingzhou.
White hair, no way to promise my return.
This visitor is leaving, don't sigh,
Your host too is a visitor.[247]

Our beds next to each other, how peacefully *you you*,[248]
The night rain sobbing, how sadly *xiao se*.
You rise to break a branch off the paulownia tree,
To give it to me for my journey of a thousand *li*.
When I return, you will know how I am,
Don't forget your feeling of this moment.

---

[244] A friend of the poet, with whom Su Shi frequently exchanged poems.
[245] Su Shi's brother.
[246] The poet is addressing to the tree.
[247] Meaning a sojourner on earth.
[248] Now, speaking to Ziyou, his brother.

THE FIRST FULL MOON OF NEW YEAR

Two years ago, I escorted the royal carriage,
The Xuande Pavilion, lanterns on ten thousand branches.
The moon, jade disc, hanging on the gate,
The stars, pearls, along the roof-ridge.
Last year, Dingzhou,
Infirmities from old age, still I had fun through the night,
The guards' banners flying, I paraded through the night streets,
The armored horses, the sounds of the hooves breaking the spring ice.
This year, Huizhou, by the south sea.[249]
This hermitage, I sojourn by the mountain monks.
Still I see torches rise
From the pine wood repeatedly.
I stroll in a palm grove,
The forest sparse, moonlight runs riot.
The magistrate's banquet over,
The flutes and drums disappear into the pine hill.
Some wild fellows show up, demanding drink,
Quickly several bushels.
Singing aloud, they leave,
I too return half drunk.

HELD UP BY HEAD WINDS AT ZIHUJIA, five poems

(2)
My return home in this life is getting ever more uncertain,
Countless green mountains, waves hit the sky.
Still here a small boat comes selling cakes,
Glad to learn there is a hamlet before the mountain.

---

[249] The poet has been banished to Huizhou , near the present-day Guangzhou, in the south.

RHYMING WITH TAO YUANMING'S "RETURN TO GARDEN AND FIELD," six poems, with a prefatory note

On the Fourth Day of Third Month, I visited Fojiyan in Baishui Shan. I bathed at the hot spring, dried my hair in the sun under a waterfall, and returned singing aloud. Riding on a palanquin, I reached the shore of Lizipu without realizing it, as I had been talking to my companion. The evening light was pale, the bamboo grove still. Lichee nuts were hanging in clusters like water chestnuts. An elderly man of eighty-five, pointing at them, said, "When they get ready to eat, please come with wine for a visit." Delighted, I promised to do so. Returning home, I took a nap. When I was awake, I heard my son, Guo, recite Tao Yuanming's "Returning to Garden and Field, six poems." Thereupon, I composed poems rhyming with them. Earlier, when I was living in Guangling, I wrote poems rhyming with his twenty poems of "Drinking Wine." Now I have done the same. In the future I intend to keep on working until I have composed poems rhyming with all of his.

(2)
The desperate monkey has fled to the forest,
The tired horse is released from a bridle for the first time.
My mind, free of worries, filled with fresh joys,
The surroundings, now familiar, enter my dreams.
River gulls, getting tamer, flock around me,[250]
Older natives of the region already come for visits.
Green lotus leaves appear in the south pond,
Purple bamboo shoots growing in the north hill.
Di-hu in the air, how would they know about wine drinking?[251]
At times this funny name brings me a smile.
Spring river, a beautiful line comes to my head,
Drunk, I drop it in the shore-less waters.

---

[250] Cf. p. 73, n105.
[251] *Di-hu*, a species of water birds, literally means "bring (wine) jug." Hence, the poet's question.

TWENTY-NINTH DAY, THIRD MONTH, two poems
(2)
Outside the gate, the orange-tree flowers are bright white,
Over the fence, lichees already ripe, speckled.
Dark is the forest, the grass tall, no man around. What a time!
I roll up the screen, raise the pillow, and from bed watch the
    mountains.

THREE JOYS IN EXILE, three poems[252]

(1) To Rise and Dress Hair in the Morning
Sweet sleep, the sea in its natural motion,
In peace the tide reaches the yellow palace.[253]
Dawn, the sun hasn't dried dew yet,
The dense pine trees, frosted and misty.
The old comb, obedient to me for years,
Allows fresh breeze through its sparse teeth.
Wash myself, awakening the ears and eyes,
Xi xi breathe the ten thousand pores.
When young, an incorrigible over-sleeper,
Always in great haste to attend the morning audience at court.
Don't say scratching is good enough,
Already I was suffering from the headdress weighing down.
Any different from a horse hitched to the shafts,
Whose flying mane filled with sand and dust?
Its ornate saddle, its crescent bit clinking,
In fact, no different from shackles,
From which no release may be expected.
A dry willow stick, where to find it so easily?[254]

---

[252] Written in 1097, during his exile on Hainan Island.

[253] In these first two lines, the poet is referring to the Daoist practice of abdominal respiration. Here he uses the Daoist terms for abdomen and the top of brain: [*qi-*] *hai* ("[breath] sea") and *huang-gong* ("yellow palace"). His meaning: "breathing naturally rises from the abdomen,/ reaches the top of the brain in perfect peace."

[254] A dry willow stick to scratch an itchy spot. Note the earlier line about scratching.

Who can write about this joy
And present it to gold-sashed ministers?

(2) To Sleep Sitting at Noon
Sit cross-legged on a reed mat,
The elbows at the bamboo armrests.
Once this posture ripens,
You enter the state of nothing-whatsoever.
Mind and body, both invisible,
Breath after breath, peaceful and long.
From the beginning no snake hides in sleep,
For what do you need hook and hand?
The mind concentrated as in midnight *chan*,
The body at ease, better than after early-morning wine.
My life has a fixed length,
My emolument has ceased, my years remaining for nothing.
An old willow tree no longer flies catkins,
But its vigor reviving, turns back decaying.
You may call this state of mine awakening,
No objects affect me.
You may say I am in a dream,
By nature this mind is free of dust.
Neither dreaming nor awakening,
Ask Master Xiyi.[255]

(3) To Wash Feet before Sleep at Night
Once Changan had a year of big snow,
But people had bundles of wood to burn, coverlets and nightwear
    to hug.

----

[255] Chen Tuan, a recluse during the early Northern Song. A visitor asks him: "I have come to see you, Master. But you are still asleep, not awake. Is there Dao also in sleep? Xiyi: "Common people recognize nothing important, they only value a state of sleep important. All humanity regards it as vital. With them the soul is gone, the spirit no longer active. They are awake, yet aware of nothing. Craving never ceasing, their [desiring] minds work harder and harder. One can't help laughing. In the realm of dust, they don't realize the dream's being a dream."

The town of Yunan had no well for drink,
So people tolerated a hundred worries for a bushel of water.
Now I have taken refuge in this desolate valley,
Owls hooting from the distant fort.
Acquiring rice is like acquiring pearls,
I dare not leave vegetable food unfinished.
But here comes the sound of pine wind,
Sou sou, the boiling noise of water in the cooking pot.
An earthen washbowl deep enough to reach my knees,
From time to time I pour in cold or warm water.
Making the lamp brighter, I cut my nails,
I feel exhilarated like a released falcon soaring.
The sky is low, clouds heavy, carrying malaria,
The land's edge near, the sea air rising.
No medicine for a swollen foot in this region,
You can cure it only with water boiled on firewood.[256]
Besides, who would wrap it with cloth for me?
I would look like a monkey in a man's outfit.

SLEEPLESS NIGHT

Sleepless on pillow, tired of long night,
The small window refuses to get bright.
A desolate village, a dog barks,
The moon going down, some people passing?
My thinning hair has long been white,
My traveling mind naturally clear, free of seeking,
Abandoned fields, crickets chirping,
Empty shuttling,[257] what would come of it?

---

[256] A practical reason for Su's nightly footbath?
[257] Refers to the crickets' noise-making.

STAYING OVERNIGHT AT JINGXINGYUAN AFTER RAIN

Grass sandals don't tread the yard of honor and profit.
A light boat, a lone leaf, floating on the open sea.
In the midst of a forest, I am in bed, listening to the night rain,
Stillness, no light to illumine the desolation.

AWAKE AT MOON-LIT NIGHT ON THE RIVERSIDE
OF TENGZHOU, Dedicated to Master Shao, one poem

The moon on the river illumines my mind,
The river water cleanses my liver.[258]
As if a pearl, no bigger than an inch in diameter,
The white jade disc on the water.
My mind is by nature like this,
The moon full, the river calm.
Who is up and dancing?
Don't make it a party of three watching.[259]
This south of the Five Mountain Ranges is malaria-infested,
Yet the moon shines cold over this river.
Thus one knows, between heaven and earth
Who wouldn't enjoy cleanness and peace?
At the head of bed a jug of wine,
Filled to the rim, like white dew about to drip.
Alone get drunk, alone get sober.
The night air, clear, pervades everywhere.
I call Master Shao,
Take the lute and play it under moonlight.
Let us together ride in a boat,
Go down the rapids of Cangwu tonight.

---

[258] The liver, believed to be the organ of feelings.
[259] Cf. Li Bai's poem, "Drink Alone under Moon Light." In the poem, Li Bai sings: "Raising a cup I welcome the bright moon./ Sitting with my shadow, a party of three."

32. LU YOU (1125–1209)

ON THE ROAD TO WANGJIANG

Am I on the wrong road? I find myself in this wild prairie.[260]
The Yangzi surging like this, where am I to go?
I rise in the wake of the magpie's first flight,
Lodge when the cows and sheep are about to come down.
The wind getting stronger, the sail tauter,
The sound of the scull constantly breaks in the sad honking of
    the geese.
Dusk coming, again I get on the Huainan road.
The trees red, the mountains blue, just right for a poem.

VISIT TO THE VILLAGE WEST OF THE MOUNTAIN

Don't laugh at the turbidity of the year-end drink at a farm house.
Bumper year, plenty of chicken and pork, enough to treat a guest.
Hill after hill, stream after stream, is the path going to disappear?
Willows dark, flowers bright, again another village.
Flutes and drums following, the spring festival is approaching,
The villagers wear simple clothes, the old custom still remaining.
From now on, if they welcome my visit on a moonlit night,
I shall carry my cane at any time and knock at the door.

STAYING OVERNIGHT BY THE MAPLE BRIDGE

For seven years I haven't visited the Maple Bridge Temple,[261]
This visitor in bed, the midnight bell, as in the past.

---

[260] The poet is on his way to Longxing , to which he is being transferred from
Zhenjiang. In the opening line, Lu You is probably asking himself about his life
in general, rather than this particular road.
[261] I.e., Hanshan Temple by the bridge.

This moonlit night doesn't quite touch my heart,
The Ba Mountains still ten thousand *li* away.[262]

GONG'AN

The land wide open, the Yangzi touches the sky,
The sandy shore eroding, the town has moved.
Avoiding the wind, the ship stops for half a day,
A man sent to buy rice, we wait for hours,
A butterfly, cold, sits on a water-oat leaf,
The gulls, tamed, float near the scull tip.
This is an old hero's place of victory,
Scratching my head, I mourn my decline.

A FARM HOUSE IN YUECHI

Late spring, the farmhouse is not yet done with tilling,
In the field the farmer goads on a pair of yellow calves.
The dirt has softened, no more clumps, the water turns sludgy,
A fine rain leaves its trace, the shoots bright green.
The green shoots transplanted, a beautiful season,
The country is in peace, no corvée being levied.
The farmer buys flowers to celebrate the wedding at the west house,
Brings wine to the east neighbor to congratulate on the birth of
   a child.
Who says farmers are outmoded?
His young daughter makes up her eyebrows in city fashion.
Her white hands nobody recognizes,
The whole village empties, all calling each other to see her
   spinning silk.
Farmhouse, farmhouse, joyous, joyous!
Not to compare with the city's mean aggressiveness.
Away from home for government work, how much have I gained?
It's been three years since I last tilled in spring.

---

[262] The Ba Mountains are in the eastern part of Sichuan Province. The poet is
on his way to Kuizhou in the province, to which he has been transferred. He
will spend eight years in that mountainous region.

FINE RAIN ON THE WAY TO JIANMEN

On my clothes, road dust over wine stains,
A long way from home, no place has failed to move my spirit.
Shouldn't I be a poet?
Fine rain, riding a donkey, I am entering Jianmen Shan.

SIT AT DAWN

Low pillow, alone in bed, night air lingering,
I sit up with a robe over the shoulders, silent, forgetting words.
Flowers in the vase, losing strength, fall without wind,
The hearth, ashes deep, warm till dawn.
The empty wardrobe, I hear a mouse gnawing from time to time,
The small window, I see crows fly by one by one.
Out of blue, I recall my recluse days,
I would get the couch down for my visitor before opening the gate
    by the water's edge.

LODGING AT THE POST

A quiet town, this old post with a red gate,
Again back in this post, I rest in an empty room, fixing my
    travel clothes.
For its flight of ninety thousand *li*, the *Kun* turns into a *Peng*,[263]
After over a thousand years, the crane returns to its old home.[264]
Going around the yard, I count the bamboo, many new shoots,
Taking off my belt, I measure the pine, its girth has grown.
On the wall only a few lines of a poem,
Dust collecting, the black ink fading, yet readable.

---

[263] Reference to the fable of a *kun*, a giant fish, flying to the south, after turning itself into a giant bird, *peng*, in the *Zhuangzi*, Ch. 1.
[264] Reference to a story of an immortal (Ding Lingwei), returning to his old town as a crane, after over a thousand years of absence.

DEEP ALEEP ON A BOAT AFTER A SHOWER

On a boat, a shower chases away a buzzing fly.
My headpiece half off, I doze off asleep in a wicker chair.
I wake up from a cool dream, twilight already at the window.
I hear some rowing voice, the boat sails down to Baling quietly.

SMALL GARDEN, four poems

(1)
The small garden in mist, the grass touches the neighbor's land,
The mulberry trees dense, the narrow path passes sideways.
Lying, I read Tao Yuanming's poems. Before finishing the book,
Again fine rain. Thereupon I go out to plow the melon patch.

(3)
South of the village, north of the village, pigeons calling rain,
Water in rice paddies full and level, new shoots stick up,
I wandered to the sky's edge, tens of thousands *li* away,
Back, I am learning spring-planting from village fathers.

AFTER SAILING PAST FANJIANG, REST AND MEAL
AT A FARM HOUSE

For a meal on the road, what would prevent relishing a bracken dish?
Evening light, I knock on the door of a farmhouse.
Xiao xiao, my short sideburns forlorn, early autumn cool,
An empty village, desolate, hungry, year in, year out.
The knotweed-grown shore, a boat poles in, geese fly up, surprised,
The marsh misty, the sound of the flute calling buffaloes.
Poetic sentiments well over at the sight of hard life,
Staggering in life isn't necessarily a loss.

VEGETABLE GARDEN, seven *jueju*

(2)

A new straw raincoat I bought with a hundred coins,
I don't envy a long gold-inlaid sash.
Dead willow trees on the dike, a sudden shower,
Shall I ask someone to draw me coming home with a plow on
    my shoulder?

A BREIF RAIN AFTER TRANSPLANTING FLOWERS,
DELIGHTED, I COMPOSE TWENTY WORDS[265]

I sit alone, at ease, doing nothing whatsoever,
Burn incense, chant a short poem.
How lovely this cool night rain,
Right after a flower planting!

REACH THE EAST CANAL, SAILING ON THE LAKE, three poems

(1)

Spring water, six or seven *li*,
Evening sun, three or four houses.
Children tend geese and ducks,
Women look after mulberry trees and hemp.
This remote place, their clothes old-fashioned,
Bumper year, laughing and chatter fill the air.
An old man ties a small boat,
Half drunk, picks wisteria flowers.

BUY A PAIR OF CLOGS

Rain one day, mud three days,
Mud dries, rain again.

---

[265] I.e., twenty characters—five in each of the four lines.

My going out hindered each time,
Which makes me miserable.
For a hundred coins I buy a pair of clogs,
Everyday I walk around the village.
East roads, north alleys,
Rain or shine, unhindered.
Why shouldn't these green sandals be beautiful?
Granted they don't last long.
Some day I will walk in deep snow
To have a drink by the lake bridge.

EAST VILLAGE, two poems

(1)
A farmer knows I go out rarely. Seeing me pass by,
He stops his plowing hands, his wife comes down from her loom.
They dig out arrowhead bulbs and cook them just right for me,
Cordially, offer me a drink to keep me from cold on my way home.

PASS MOUNTAIN VILLAGES, DISPENSING MEDICINES, five poems

(1)
During my stroll, I happen to come to this mountain village again,
An old villager, blocking my way, stops me to share a jug of his wine.
When I met you last time, sir, my grandson was not yet one year old,
Now he can already look after chickens and pigs.

(3)
A boy, supporting an old man, is waiting for me by the creek,
Coming to me, he says the man has long been suffering from a
    headache with no relief.
No need to seek *chuanxiong*, *baizhi*, [266] or anything of the sort.
Let him read my poems. When done, his headache will go away
    by itself.

---

[266] Both medicinal plants.

(4)
I always go, carrying medicines on a donkey's shoulders.
On village alleys, people welcome me from both sides.
All tell me, you cured me in the past,
When a child is born, many name it "Lu"[267]

EARLY WINTER, eight poems

(3)
When young, I loved books, nothing else interested me,
Food is getting cold, meat dry, someone calling. I wouldn't go.
All my life I was in the wrong, never awaking,
In old age, I have become a bookworm, ah, how sad!

THE CHEN GARDEN, two poems

(1)
Slanting sunlight on the city wall, the painted horn[268] pensive,
The Chen Garden, pond and terrace, no longer as they once were.
My sad heart, under the bridge, rippling waves spring green,
Long ago, they reflected her dazzling figure.[269]

(2)
The dream was cut short, her fragrance vanished, forty years ago,
The old willows in the garden no longer fly their cotton.

---

[267] The poet's name.
[268] Announcing the hour of day.
[269] The poet is thinking of his first wife, Tang Wan, whom he loved but was forced to divorce because of his mother's rejection of her daughter-in-law. The poem indicates that the couple had visited the Chen Garden during their marriage. Lu You was seventy-four years old when he wrote this poem. Apparently, he had met Tang Wan once again in this garden after their divorce; then she, remarried, was with her husband. Soon after, she dies. Lu You writes a few more poems about her in his old age. One of them, which he writes at age 80, is the next one ("During the Night of . . .").

This body will soon become dirt on the Huiji Shan,[270]
Still, I shed tears, mourning our time gone by.

DURING THE NIGHT OF SECOND DAY, TWELFTH MONTH, I DREAM STROLLING IN THE CHEN GARDEN, two poems

(1)
The road approaches the south of the city,[271] I already fear going on,
Once inside the Chen Garden, again my heart hurts.
The plum flowers are still blooming, the fragrance permeating
    my sleeves.
The temple bridge nearby soaked in green, spring water has risen.

---

[270] A mountain near Shao Xing, where he lives in his retirement.
[271] Where the Chen Garden is located.

33. GAO QI (1336–1374)

THE SONG OF QINGQIUZI, with a prefatory note

There is a green hill by the river. I have moved to the south of the hill.[272]
So I call myself Qinqiuzi [Green-hill-man]. Idly, doing nothing, all day
I work on composing poems. I compose "Song of Qinqiuzi" to express
my thought, to dispel the mockery of poetry debauchery.

Qingqiuzi, thin and pure,
Originally a celestial official in the palace of five-hued clouds,
Some years ago, exiled down to this world.
To people he doesn't give his name.
Though he wears his clogs, he doesn't travel far,
He carries a hoe, but loathes digging.
Though he has a sword, he lets it rust away,
Though he has books, he leaves them scattered around.
He refuses to bow for five bushels of grain,[273]
Refuses to use his tongue to bring to surrender seventy walled
    cities.[274]

He only loves to find poetic lines.
Reciting poems, answering them in rhyme himself,
He wanders in the field, cane in his hand, rope around his waist,
His onlookers, not knowing him, laugh.
They call him an obtuse scholar of Lu,[275]
Or a crazy student of Chu.

---

[272] This hill is located by the Wusongjiang River, outside Suzhou.
[273] Allusion to Tao Yuanming's statement: "Would I bow [before a county official] for five bushels of grain. . . ?"
[274] Allusion to the historical incident in which Li Shiqi of the Han made the seventy walled cities of Qi surrender through his eloquence.
[275] I.e.., Confucian scholar.

Hearing this, Qinqiuzi doesn't mind it at all,
His reciting sound, ah and oh never ending.
Reciting in the morning, he forgets his hunger,
Reciting in the evening, he dissipates his unhappiness.

When absorbed in working on a poem,
He seems unaware of anything else, as if drunk,
His hair, no time to comb,
Household matters, beyond his attention.
The child cries, he doesn't know how to calm it,
A guest arrives, he fails to receive him properly.
Never worried, though poor like Hui,[276]
Never envious of Yi Dun's wealth,[277]
Never ashamed of his coarse clothes,
Never covetous of a bright cap ribbon[278],
Never asking about the dragon-tiger fight,[279]
Never concerned with the race between the crow and rabbit.[280]

Alone he sits by the riverside, facing the water,
Alone he strolls in the wood.
He quarries the primordial energy, searching for the cosmic essence,
The ten thousand things[281] find it hard to hide from him their secrets.
He exercises his mental power throughout the vast universe,
Sitting quiet, he makes the formless speak. His mind
So fine, as if it could smash a flea hanging from a cow's tail,
So powerful, as if it could slaughter a giant whale,
So clear, as if it had drunk heavenly dew,
So sharp, as if to cut open craggy peaks.

---

[276] Confucius's disciple.

[277] A man of Lu with great wealth during the Spring–Autumn period.

[278] Of a high official.

[279] I.e., between contenders for power.

[280] The three-legged crow on the sun and the rabbit on the moon in the ancient myth. Their "race" refers to the progression of time.

[281] An idiom meaning "all things of the universe/world".

The dark clouds opening, the blue sky appears,
The frozen ground thawing, new buds sprout.[282]

Climbing the column of heaven, he searches the caves of the moon,
The torch burning in a rhinoceros horn, he shines on all the monsters
    of Mt. Niuzhu.
His wondrous imagination, suddenly inspired by the spirits,
Beautiful scenes compete with rivers and hills,
Stars and rainbows intensify their brilliance,
Mist and fog nourish flowers.
To his ears all sounds heavenly music,
To his taste all foods as if at a great feast.

Nothing of this world an object of joy for me,
I produce for myself bells and chimes to make sounds.
Over this thatch-roofed house by the river, windy rain clears up,
The door shut, enough sleep, now I have finished a poem.
Beating a pot, I sing it aloud,
I don't care if it disturbs worldly ears.
I wish I could call the old man of Jun Shan to have him bring his long
    flute given to him by the heavenly immortals,[283]
And play it accompanying my song under moonlight.

But the sudden raging of waves on the river, I fear,
Frightened cries of birds and beasts, and mountain quakes.[284]
Hearing of all this, God on High, furious,
Would send down a white crane to recall me.
Not tolerating any mischief in this world,
He would have me wear a flying belt and get me back to his
    jade capital.

---

[282] The meaning of the last two lines is unclear.

[283] Jun Shan is an island in the Dongting Lake. According to legend, an old man on this island was given once by heavenly beings various flutes which they had themselves used before. The playing of these flutes was said to have caused all kinds of prodigious phenomena to take place.

[284] Caused by the old man's playing of the heavenly instruments.

LYING IDLY ON A RAINY DAY

The bed leaning to the screen, the desk standing obliquely,
I lie watching the new swallows arrive at this poor house.
This idle life, my mind hazy, nothing occupies it,
Seeing the rain, I only worry apricot flowers being ruined.

VISITING MASTER HU THE RECLUSE

Crossing water, and again crossing water,
Gazing at flowers, and again gazing at flowers.
Spring wind, along the river path,
I have reached your house without realizing.

WHENCE MY MELANCHOLY?

Whence my melancholy?
Autumn arriving, I see it come.
I want to express it, but hard to name it,
Though vague, I am fully aware of it.
Anxious, do I fear getting old?
Restless, do I deplore this mean existence?
Certainly not a poor scholar's moaning,
Would it rather be an exile's sadness?
Do you say I think of the day of my return?
But I have never left my home village.
Do you say my parting with someone?
But I have never parted with a dear one.

At first, I compared this melancholy to creepers,
Evening dew wouldn't wilt it away.
I also compared it to mist,
Autumn wind wouldn't blow it away.
Rising between my mind and eyes,
It arrives fast, departs rather slowly,
I wonder how long this melancholy
Will still linger on?

In the past I lived by the west brook,
Enjoying the beauty of mountains and rivers.
Now, returning to the east garden,
I grieve the withering of plants all the more.
This life of seclusion, who would visit me?
Only melancholy accompanies me.
People love merry-making greatly,
Playing, reveling, they never get tired of it.
I alone, carrying this melancholy,
Roam. What am I to do?[285]

---

[285] Cf. the following lines from the *Dao De Jing* (Ch. 20):
Everybody is cheerful,
As if enjoying a great feast;
As if going up to the terrace for the Spring Festival.
I alone am unexcited, giving no sign,
Like a baby who has not yet smiled;
Weary, nowhere to return.
Everybody has more than enough,
I alone am dispossessed.
Mine is the mind of an ignorant man.
How indifferent!
Common folks are bright,
I alone am dark.
They are keen,
I alone am dull.
Adrift, I feel as if on the open sea,
Blown by a high wind that seems never to come to rest.
Everybody is put to use,
I alone am stubborn and foolish like a boar.
Alone, different from others, I treasure the nursing mother.

Appendix 1
"Oh, Let Me Return!"[286]

Perhaps, the phrase *"gui qulai xi"* is one of the few poetic phrases from the fourth-century China that have survived in the popular memory till the present day. Recently, I googled it and read on one Chinese music website the following passage with the heading "Come Away Home/ *Gui Qu Lai Ci*":

> The lyrics for this melody are a famous poem by Tao Qian (Tao Yuanming, 365–427). . . .
> The melody of *Gui Qu Lai Ci* is still popular today. A poem by Lu You (1125–1210) suggests the lyrics were sung in connection with *qin* at least at the 12th century, but no description is given of the melody. This, the earliest surviving occurrence in music form, is clearly identifiable with the modern version, though there are quite a few differences. Versions survive in at least 29 handbooks to 1961, with most including, with slight variations, the same lyrics. . . .
> The poem has also been used as the inspiration for several paintings.[287]

I find this passage quite interesting, though some of the information contained seems confusing. From what I read in it, however, I gather that Tao's poem has found its way into the world of music since its earliest days and survived until today (?) in the memory of the Chinese people in some form or other, not so much because of any "melody" accompanying it, as because of the poem itself (the "lyrics") that has appealed to the Chinese mind. What is in it that has made it survive for over fifteen centuries? I think the inquiry into this question may illuminate something—perhaps something significant—about the social history of China. That is, of course, not the issue I intend to pursue here; mine is a very modest one. The heading of the above-cited passage is "Come Away Home." I wonder if this is the way the lovers of the "lyrics," particularly in later times, took the phrase "*gui qulai xi*" to mean. If so, that seems to indicate that they have not grasped the original sense of "self-urging" implied in Tao Yuanming's phrase. What do I mean by "self-urging"? This is what I want to discuss here.

Central to our problem is the two-character compound word "*qu-lai*," of which the first character, "*qu*," used alone, means "to go" while the second one, "*lai*," again alone, means "to come"—two characters referring to two opposite movements. When "*qu-lai*" is thus read merely as the combination of the two characters, it would simply mean "to leave and come." Now, in Tao's phrase the compound word "*qu-lai*" is preceded by "*gui*," which by itself means "to return," so that the three characters in succession literally could be taken to mean "return/ go/ come."[288] But how is one supposed to make sense of this puzzling sequence? The heading of the quoted passage, "come away home" suggests one way of "solving" the puzzle, namely, taking "*gui*" to mean "(to return) home," "*qu*" "(to go) away," and "*lai*" "to come." But so understood, the phrase would be an awkward way of saying simply "come home." This cannot possibly be Tao's meaning, for he is not telling someone else to "come home"; rather, he is expressing what goes through his own mind, thinking of returning home.

As I suggested in the Preface, his meaning is quite straightforward. We have a problem here only because the original sense of the idiom "*qu-lai*" has been lost in common usage. Two Japanese scholars, in their co-authored translation/commentary of Tao Yuanming's poetry,[289] point out that during the Eastern Jin period (317–420), when Tao lived, the compound "*qu-lai*" as an idiom merely expressed the speaker's *urging* of an action, without meaning anything the characters themselves meant separately. In support of their contention, the authors cite the following sentence from the section on Recluse Qi Jia in the *Book of Jin*: "*yin qulai, yin qulai*" ("let us withdraw, let us withdraw").[290] When "*qu-lai*" is so understood as an expression of urging, Tao's phrase "*gui qu-lai*" should be read to mean something like "let us return." [291]

However, this reading must be modified somewhat in view of the fact that the person to be urged to "return" in the poem is actually the poet himself, not any collectivity ("us"). Hence my reading of the phrase as "let *me* return." It must be pointed out that this is perfectly consistent with Chinese usage, in which the phrase *"gui qu-lai"* is used quite neutrally in grammatical terms; that is, as far as the *person* and *number* of the phrase is concerned, the idiom is used without indicating whether the object of the urging is a collective "us" or a personal "me." As the poem reads, in the opening stanza he is telling himself that he has enslaved himself already too long away from home, and *urging* himself that he should return to his "field and garden," before they turn "wild."

A few words about the structure of this famous poem. The poem has four stanzas, of which the first and the third open with the phrase "Oh, let me return!" Structurally, this seems to suggest that the poem was written *before* his departure for home. Furthermore, the second line in the first stanza reads: "Field and garden are about to turn into wilderness, why not return?" Here, clearly, he is *urging* himself to return. On the other hand, he is already on his way home in the latter part of the same stanza. (After all, the poet's own prefatory note tells us that it was written after he had quit the job.) Indeed, the remaining stanzas include not only a description of his homecoming but also his happy days now back home. In the third stanza, Tao even mentions the arrival of the following spring, even though he begins again with "Oh, let me return." All this may sound confusing to the reader. How are we then to comprehend the poem as a whole? I read this poem as Tao's song of joy back in the country *after* the eighty some days of misery at Pengze. The joy he describes is not just the joy of living in the country, but that of having "returned" from that place of misery. By repeating the phrase "Oh, let me return!" the poet is indicating this *special* joy, which is the context of the poem. In this sense, one may read the phrase *gui qulai* as a sort of refrain. When so read, the feeling of the discrepancy between the phrase and the contents of the poem may disappear, and the poem as a whole may be read as an expression of the poet's joyous return home from his lost days away.

Appendix 2
Images beyond Syntax

The poet has the license to go against the ordinary way of speech, even violating the syntax of the language she uses. Why this license? Indeed, a creative poet often violates even the very poetic tradition to which she belongs, producing her own style. Is there some necessity in all this? I believe there is. In this essay, I want to discuss these and other related issues concerning poetry's departure from the established conventions of expression.

In the latter part of the Preface, I referred to what Professor W-L Yip calls the "syntactically uncommitted" nature of imagery in Chinese poetry. In my view, this "uncommitted" nature of images is not something peculiarly Chinese but, strictly speaking, something common to all images, in the way they come to the perceiver. In other words, the images, whether in our actual sense perception or imagination, always present themselves to us "syntactically uncommitted." But let us first briefly review Professor Yip's notion of the "syntactically uncommitted[ness]" of images. In a Chinese poem, he points out, images are often "juxtaposed," so that the syntax doesn't tell us what sort of relation they have. As an example, he discusses the famous first line of Du Fu's "Spring View": "*guo po shan he zai*".[292] This line may be translated, word-by-word: "country/ broken/ mountain/ river/ remain," but somewhat poetically:

(A) "The country in ruin, mountains and rivers remain as ever."

Notice that (A) gives us two images ("the country in ruin" and "mountains and rivers remaining the same") juxtaposed but doesn't tell us how they are related, say, in terms of contrast—that is, syntactically. Yip cites the following English translation of the line, in which the relation is supplied by the translator:

(B) Though a country be sundered, hills and rivers endure.²⁹³

In (B) the syntax does present the two images in terms of contrast, thanks to the conjunctive "though." Yip's point is that where two or more images are "syntactically uncommitted" in the original poem, the translator shouldn't supply their relation by way of such words as "though," "but" and "as." His complaint is not simply that to do so would be to inject an interpretive element in the translation. His reason is more fundamental. Felicitously, he compares the juxtaposition of two images in Chinese poems to the "juxtaposition of two separate shots" in the montage technique in the film. This comparison is illuminating. Just as the viewer of a film is expected to catch the meaning (or relation) of juxtaposed scenes without being told, so the reader of a poem is to recognize the relation of juxtaposed images without being so told. Referring to Du Fu's first line (in the original), Yip writes:

> The reader feels, *without being told*, the content and tension in the scenery so presented, and the introduction of explanatory elaboration will destroy the immediate contact between the viewer and the scene, as in the case of this typical translation [(B) cited above] and many others. (Italics in text)²⁹⁴

In essence, I agree with Professor Yip on this point. However, I recognize the "syntactically uncommitted" images, not just in Chinese poetry, but in our perceptual experience in general. With this recognition, I shall broadly discuss, in what follows, the creative aspect of poetry. Suppose I see before me two cats, black and white, and notice their contrast in color. In this case, do I actually *perceive* their contrasting relation, in terms of sensory experience? Of course not. What I perceive are two images, an image of black cat and an image of white cat. Their contrasting relation is what I recognize in what I perceive. To put it in another way, it is I who "relates" them by way of contrast. This is not to say that I do the relating consciously or thinkingly. Indeed, I may *feel as if* I were actually "perceiving" the relation as much as the images themselves. That is, phenomenologically, one may say, I do "see" their contrast.

Let us return to Du Fu's *"guo po shan he zai."* Suppose someone reads it as a prose sentence, without realizing its source. In this case, it is quite conceivable that the reader reads it simply as a matter-of-fact statement: "The country is broken, and mountains and rivers remain the same." Would the reading comprehension of this statement of fact require the reader's *imaging* of the country broken and mountains and rivers remaining the same? Most unlikely, and, at any event, not necessarily. For prose reading generally takes place at a *conceptual* level; that is, the mind moves from idea (or concept) to idea, not from image to image. Accordingly, there is no way that this prose reader should recognize (or "perceive") the contrasting relation of the two *images*. This is, of course, not to suggest that the reader would be incapable of recognizing any relation of contrast even at the *conceptual* level. However, the recognition of a relation between *images* is one thing, and the recognition of a relation at a *conceptual* level is another.

I have asserted that prose reading generally takes place at a conceptual level.[295] I should like to return to this sweeping pronouncement. But first, a few broad observations. The language of prose is typically that of our everyday speech. In this sense, we may call it the language of our everyday universe. This language is at the same time our everyday conceptual framework, insofar as, in our everyday life, we not only think but also see things around us through its network, so to say. In this sense, we may say that our everyday perception as well as our everyday thinking conforms to the syntax of our everyday language, which is the language of prose. This is the way we think and see "things" in prose, as it were. Here I am speaking of seeing "things," as opposed to "seeing images." Again, in our everyday life, "things" that we see are namable things, i.e., things that have their place within our conceptual universe. For this reason, these are abstract. What is it to see an apple on the table? In our busy everyday life, it means hardly more than subsuming what the eye perceives under the concept of apple, a conceptual activity. At work in this is the *thinking* mind, not the *seeing* or *imaging* mind.[296]

When we speak of a line in a poem in terms of syntax, we are ultimately speaking of it in view of our everyday language. But a poetic line is intended to arouse images in the reader's mind; and it is not to be read simply conceptually. Hence, the question of whether or not a line in a poem violates any syntactical rule is simply out of place. In my opening paragraph, I asked why the poet's license to violate syntactical rules? There isn't really the question of her having or not having such a license; the poet is simply *above* syntax. Indeed, her transcendence of ordinary language is a necessity, not a matter of license. So often the poet can arouse the reader's mind from its thinking mode to the imaging mode only by following the way of images, against the dictate of the abstract network of her language. Yes, a creative poet often violates not only the rules of her language but also the conventions of her own poetic tradition. Why? The reason is fundamentally the same. Generally, again, the world of conventions, whether it is of a linguistic or a poetic tradition, is the world where the past rules. The poet may find that the poetic tradition of the past is not adequate to present her own poetic vision.

What I have said about the poet's creative process may suggest something fundamental about the nature of poetic experience, from the standpoint of the reader, also. Simply put, poetic experience must be that of the imaging mind. In reading Du Fu's *"guo po shan he zai,"* the reader experiences the images of the country in ruin and mountains and rivers remaining the same, and also "perceives" their contrast. In this article I have spoken of the relation of images primarily in terms of contrast, but needless to say, what is true of contrast in imagery is essentially true of such other relations as "resemblance," "parallelism," "congruity," "incongruity," and "irony." Their relations must be "perceived" in terms of images, not just recognized conceptually or abstractly. Only then can one speak of poetic experience. Otherwise, there may be intellectual understanding, but not experience.

As I close, I would like to cite one passage from Gaston Bachelard:

> One must be receptive, receptive to the image at the moment it appears: if there be a philosophy of poetry, it must appear and reappear through a significant verse, in total adherence to an isolated image; to be exact, in the very ecstasy of the newness of the image. The poetic image is a sudden salience on the surface of the psyche. . . .[297]

Appendix 3
Thoreau's "Mythology of the Wild"

1.

In the "Introduction" to his biography of Thoreau, Walter Harding writes that he was "most impressed by Thoreau's aliveness," and adds: "All his senses were thoroughly awake and he was able to examine the worlds of both man and nature with a keenness and clarity that have made him one of the great observers of the American scene."[298] I agree with Harding. In the first half of this essay, I explore Thoreau's aliveness, first, in terms of wakefulness to the life of nature, then more in existential terms, referring to the joy of living in nature. In the remainder of the essay, I shall discuss broadly Thoreau's nature writing, especially in light of his "mythology" of the wild, and his "gospel" of the present moment. In his essay, "Walking," Thoreau writes: "Life consists in wildness. The most alive is the wildest."[299] At the outset, it should be noted that the sort of life he speaks of is life in its primordial sense—that is, the sort which we humans share in common with all our fellow creatures. Perhaps, it may not be an exaggeration to say that this is the root idea of his criticisms of many aspects of civilization.

Thoreau writes on various subjects in his *Journal* and other writings. Even in *Walden* his subjects are not limited to his experiment in life in the woods. But still, central to his records of his observations in nature is his joy of just being in his "society" of the wild, alive to its ever-changing scenes and hearing its ever-present music. Let us read the opening paragraph of "Sounds" in *Walden*, the chapter which follows the one on "Reading":

But while we are confined to books, though the most select and classic, and read only particular written languages, which are themselves but dialects and provincial, we are in danger of forgetting the language which all things and events speak without metaphor, which alone is copious and standard. The rays which stream through the shutter will be no longer remembered when the shutter is wholly removed. No method nor discipline can supersede the necessity of being forever *on the alert*. What is a course of history or philosophy or poetry, no matter how well selected . . . , compared with the discipline of looking always at what is to be *seen*? Will you be a reader, a student merely, or a *seer*? Read your fate, see what is *before you*, and walk on into futurity.[300]

To "see what is *before* you" is to be *alive* to what is presented to your senses. It means the *mind*'s presence to what is present to the *body*. Hence, "the necessity of being forever on the alert." The way we live, our minds are not always *with* our bodies, so that we more often than not fail to see what is clearly *before* our eyes. Our eyes see it, but not our minds. Here Thoreau is speaking of none other than "mindful" seeing. He sometimes discovers himself "walking merely," that is, *without attending* to what comes before his eyes. Mindless walking, mindless seeing! In one entry in the *Journal* (6/11/1851), Thoreau writes:

When you get into the road, though far from the town, and feel sand under your feet, it is as if you had reached your own gravel walk. You no longer hear the whip-poor-will nor regard your shadow, for here you expect a fellow-traveler. You catch yourself *walking merely* The road leads your steps and thoughts alike to the town. You see only the path, and your thoughts wander from the objects which are presented to your senses. You are no longer in place. . . .[301]

Why this mindless walking, mindless seeing? For our minds are constantly occupied with some thoughts or other—things that are *absent* to our senses. In "Walking," Thoreau again writes:

When we walk, we naturally go to the fields and woods: what would become of us, if we walked only in a garden or a mall? Even some sects of philosophers have felt the necessity of importing the woods to themselves, since they did not go to the woods. "They planted groves and walks of Platanes," where they took *subdiales ambulationes* in porticos open to the air. Of course it is of no use to direct our steps to the woods, if they do not carry us thither. I am alarmed when it happens that I have walked a mile into the woods bodily, without getting there in spirit. In my afternoon walk I would fain forget all my morning occupations and my obligations to society. But it sometimes happens that I cannot easily shake off the village. The thought of some work will run in my head and I am not where my body is,—I am out of my senses. . . .[302]

2.

Let us read the following passages, which immediately follow the one I cited earlier from the chapter on "Sounds" in *Walden*:

I did not read books the first summer; I hoed beans. Nay, I often did better than this. There were times when I could not afford to sacrifice the bloom of the present moment to any work, whether of the head or hands. . . . Sometimes, in a summer morning, having taken my accustomed bath, I sat in my sunny doorway from sunrise till noon, rapt in a revery, amidst the pines and hickories and sumachs, in undisturbed solitude and stillness, while the birds sang around or flitted noiseless through the house, until by the sun falling in at my west window, or the noise of some traveler's wagon on the distant highway. I was reminded of the lapse of time. I grew in those seasons like corn in the night . . . . I realized what the Orientals mean by contemplation and the forsaking of works. For the most part, I minded not how the hours went. The day advanced as if to light some work of mind; it was morning, and lo, now it is evening. . . . My days were not days of the week . . . ; for I lived like the Puri Indians, of whom it is said that "for yesterday, to-day, and to-morrow they have only one word. . . ." This was sheer idleness to my fellow-townsmen, no doubt; but if the birds and flowers had tried me by their standard, I should not have been found wanting. A man must find his occasions in himself, it is true. The natural day is very calm, and will hardly reprove his indolence.

I had this advantage, at least, in my mode of life, over those who were obliged to look abroad for amusement, to society and the theatre, that my life itself was become any amusement and never ceased to be novel. It was a drama of my scenes and without an end. . . . Housework was a pleasant pastime. When my floor was dirty, I rose early, and setting all my furniture out of doors on the grass . . . , dashed water on the floor, and sprinkled white sand from the pond on it, and then with a broom scrubbed it clean and white; and by the time the villagers had broken their fast the morning sun had dried my house sufficiently to allow me to move in again, and my meditation were almost uninterrupted. It was pleasant to see my whole household effects out on the grass, making a little pile like a gypsy's pack, and my three-legged table . . . , standing amid the pines and hickories. They seemed glad to set out themselves, and as if unwilling to be brought in. . . .[303]

These paragraphs are indeed Thoreau's records of mindful living in *Walden* and his joy from it. Perhaps one can easily imagine a mindless soul spending his days in a similar environment, without ever paying his attention to the eastern sky at daybreak, nor to the water by moonlight, nor to the chickadee's singing. In the second passage, Thoreau writes about sitting "in my sunny doorway from sunrise till noon, rapt in a revery . . , in undisturbed solitude and stillness." Isn't he speaking of the joy of mindful seeing and living? He finds it "pleasant to see my whole household effects out on the grass." Is this just the childish fun of seeing an unusual scene of his indoor objects lying or standing outdoors "like a Gypsy's pack"? No. It is his joy of seeing the contents of his nest out on the grass *happily* bathing in the sun, *as in a fairy tale*. He even sympathizes with their reluctance to go inside.

For Thoreau, being alive to nature is not simply to be observant of things in the wild. For him all inhabitants of nature are living things, including sun, moon, stars, mountains and rivers, as well as animals and plants. He is alive to their life activities, their life stories, as he observes all happenings in nature as life phenomena. His *Journal* is full of records of such observations. Read the following passages:

(5/31/50)
Today, May 31st, a red and white cow, being uneasy, broke out of the steam-mill pasture and crossed the bridge and broke into

Elijah Wood's grounds. When he endeavored to drive her out by the bars, she boldly took to the water, wading first through the meadows full of ditches, swam across the river, about forty rods wide at this time, and landed in her own pasture again. She was a buffalo crossing her Mississippi. This exploit conferred some dignity on the herd in my eyes, already dignified—and reflectedly on the river—which I looked on as a kind of Bosphorus.

I love to see the domestic animals reassert their native rights,—any evidence that they have not lost their original wild habits and vigor.[304]

(9/19/50)
There is a good echo from that wood to one standing on the side of Fair Haven. It was particularly good to-day. The woodland lungs seemed particularly sound to-day; they echoed your shout with a fuller and rounder voice than it was given in, seeming to *mouth* it. [italics in text] You had to choose the right key or pitch, else the woods would not echo it with any spirit, and so with eloquence. Of what significance is any sound if Nature does not echo it?[305]

(11/11/50)
This afternoon I heard a single cricket singing, chirping, in a bank, the only one I have heard for a long time, like a squirrel or a little bird, clear and shrill,—as I fancied, like an evening robin, singing in this evening of the year. A very fine and poetical strain for such a little singer. I had never heard the cricket so like a bird. It is a remarkable note. The earth-song.[306]

(5/21/51)
I have heard now within a few days that peculiar dreaming sound of the frogs which belong to the summer, their midsummer nights dream.[307]

. . . .

. . . .

The frog had eyed the heavens from his marsh, until his mind was filled with visions, and he saw more than belongs to this fenny earth. He mistrusted that he was become a dreamer and visionary.

Leaping across the swamp to his fellow, what was his joy and consolation to find that he too had seen the same sights in the heavens, he too had dreamed the same dreams!

From nature we turn astonished to this *near* but supernatural fact.[308] [italics in text]

3.

One can perhaps detect easily in his *Journal* and other writings Thoreau's keen feeling of *livingness* when in the wild—something which he again and again confesses missing in human society. This feeling is more than a happy awareness of this or that *particular* scene in nature; one may call it a *general*, yet *existential* consciousness, which gives one a deeper sense of aliveness. He watches the simmering reflection of the moon on the water, which gives him a certain aesthetic satisfaction. However, at the same time, it gives him also the existential affirmation of being alive: the joy of life itself. I have already cited the passage from "Walking": "Life consists in wildness. The most alive is the wildest." Let us take these words in their existential sense.

In one of his later diary entries (8/10/1857) Thoreau writes:

Aug. 10. How meanly and miserably we live for the most part! We escape fate continually by the skin of our teeth, as the saying is. We are practically desperate. What kind of gift is life unless we have spirits to enjoy it and taste its true flavor? if, in respect to spirits, we are to be forever cramped and in debt? Have the gods sent us into this world,—to this *muster*,—to do chores, hold horses, and the like, and not given us any spending money?[309] [italics in text]

Thoreau is here clearly referring to the general condition of humanity in civilization, in which he finds our sprits "cramped and in debt." What kind of joy can we experience in such a condition? In another entry (11/9/1855), he flatly states: "I hate the present modes of living and getting a living. Farming and shopkeeping and working at a trade or profession are all odious to me."[310]

Thoreau particularly disliked business. He says: "In my experience nothing is so opposed to poetry—not crime—as business. It is a negation of life."[311] In Thoreau, poetry stands for the imagination, the presence of human spirit. Accordingly, to him, the opposition to poetry amounts to the denial of the very thing which makes our living uniquely human. In the following entry (2/18/51), in fact, Thoreau equates "honest living" with "poetic" living—a passage which could be puzzling to any reader who fails to recognize the spiritual nature of being *poetic*.

> There is little or nothing to be remembered written on the subject of getting an honest living. Neither the New Testament nor the Poor Richard speaks to our condition. . . . How to make the getting our living poetic—! for if it is not poetic, it is not life but death that we get.[312]

In this same entry, Thoreau later acknowledges frankly: "The most practically important of all questions, it seems to me, is how shall I get my living?" This is quite understandable especially in view of his meager earning. Besides helping his father at his pencil-making shop, he worked from time to time as a land-surveyor for townspeople. This did take him to the fields or woods. But he complains: "[T]he least affair of that kind is as if you had [a] black veil drawn over your face which shut out nature. . . ."[313] How could he then experience the joy of life even in company of birds chirping all around him?

4.

So far I have cited quite a few passages from *Walden* and his *Journal*, some of which might have struck the reader as too fable-like or poetic. In such instances, one may wonder if he is merely carried away by his fanciful imagination. In the *Journal* (9/20/1851), he writes: "The poet must keep himself unstained and aloof. Let him perambulate the bounds of Imagination's provinces the realms of faery, and not the insignificant boundaries of towns. The excursions of the imagination are so bound-less—the limits of towns are so petty.[314] Indeed, Thoreau is not at all hesitant to "perambulate . . . the realms of faery." In one place, he writes: "I confess that I am partial to wild fancies, which transcend the order of time and development."[315] But his "fancies" are fundamentally "fancies" of life, not mere romantic flights. For him, the echoing woodland should have its lungs; the frogs too may dream their midsummer nights dream. In his fanciful records of the wild, Thoreau is not writing merely metaphorically or colorfully; rather, he is reporting his own *imaginative*, or rather, *mindful* observation of the life in the woods. We have already seen him assert in *Walden* that one ought to listen to "the language which all things and events speak without metaphor, which alone is copious and standard." It is crucial to keep in mind that Thoreau's poetic language is fundamentally not metaphorical but "mythologic," as he calls it. It is the living language of nature itself that he hears and records.

In his *Journal* (11/9/51), Thoreau mentions his brief exchange with a certain C, a fellow walker (Ellery Channing?), who, observing Thoreau scribble in his note-book, tells that "he [C] confines himself to the ideal, purely ideal remarks; he leaves the facts to me."[316] A paragraph later, Thoreau writes:

> I too would fain set down something beside facts. Facts should only be the frame to my pictures; they should be material to the mythology which I am writing. Not facts to assist men to make money—farmers to farm profitably in any common sense. Facts to tell why I am—and where I have been—or what I have thought. . . . My facts shall be falsehoods to the common sense. I would so state facts that they shall be significant, shall be myths or mythologic. Facts which the mind perceived, thoughts which the body thought,—with these I deal. I, too, cherish vague and misty forms, vaguest when the cloud at which I gaze is dissipated quite and naught but the skyey depths are seen.[317]

I find this passage illuminating; it tells us about the nature of Thoreau's literary enterprise. Let us look at it closely. The "pictures" he paints are his *imaginative* creations, to which the "facts" he observes constitute their "frame"—just as, say, Cézanne's "Mont Sainte-Victoire" is his artistic creation, to which the mountain standing is merely its "frame." Notice that these "facts" are not some impersonal, objective incidents. The "frame" is really inseparable from the "pictures" themselves, just as Mont Sainte-Victoire is from Cézanne's painting of it. To be sure, Thoreau sees his "facts" with his eyes, but his *imaginative* mind attending at the same time. They are indeed "[f]acts which the mind perceived, thoughts which the body thought." (I find this apposition of the "perceiving" mind and the "thinking" body quite revealing.[318]) So, in *Walden*, he speaks of "my own sun and my own moon and stars."[319] He does admit that *his* "facts" would be "falsehoods to the common sense," but adds, "I would so state facts that they shall be significant, shall be myths or mythologic." Notice the "facts" so *stated* would be his "pictures," which should have human significance, life meaning. Hence his "mythology" of the wild is not an objective description of nature, even in a metaphorical sense. It is a life story of nature perceived by the mind, and thought by the body. In the last sentence, Thoreau, referring back to his fellow walker's mentioning of "the ideal," asserts that he too appreciates "the ideal"—the "vague and misty forms," meaning his imaginative moments.

In his essay on "Walking," Thoreau again brings up his topic of "mythology," after noting the "tame" nature of English literature, which fails to express our "yearning for the Wild." Here he is asserting that the universe of the wild demands its *own* form of writing—namely, a "mythology" of the life of nature. Let us look at this rather broad remark. Notice once again his lament on our loss of "fancy and imagination."

> I do not know of any poetry to quote which adequately expresses this yearning for the Wild. Approached from this side, the best poetry is tame. I do not know where to find in any literature, ancient or modern, any account which contents me of that Nature which even I am acquainted. You will perceive that I demand something which no Augustan nor Elizabethan age, which no *culture*, in short, can give. Mythology comes nearer to it than anything. How much more fertile a Nature, at least, has Grecian mythology its root in than English literature! Mythology is the crop which the Old World bore before its soil was exhausted, before the fancy and imagination were affected with blight; and which it still bears, wherever its pristine vigor is unabated.[320] (italics in text)

Here Thoreau claims to find the root of Greek mythology *in nature*. I cite below an entry from his *Journal*, which may cast some light on his meaning of the "mythology" of the wild as well as on his claim about Greek mythology. (The entry is dated "Walden, April 17, 1846).")

> Even nations are ennobled by affording protection to the weaker races of animals. When I read of some custom by which an ancient people recognized the migration of birds and beasts, or any neces-

sity of theirs, they seem not more savage than more god like—
[sic] The Greeks were not above this human intercourse with
nature. They were as happy as children on the arrival of the swallow
in the spring—and the passage of cranes from the sources of the
Nile. . . .

According to Hare "The children in Rhodes greeted the latter
(i.e, the swallow) as herald of the spring in a little song. Troops of
them, carrying about a swallow (...), sang this from door to door,
and collected provisions in return." I give my own translation as
most literal.

> The swallow has come,
> The swallow has come,
> Bringing beautiful hours,
> Beautiful seasons,
> White in the belly,
> Black on the back.
> —Wilt thou bring forth figs
> From thy fat house,
> And a cup of wine,
> And a canister of cheese,
> And wheaten bread? . . . .
> . . . .
> . . . .
>   Athenaeus viii, c 60 [321]

Thoreau recognizes a *godlike*, rather than savage, mind, in an ancient
people who were "as happy as children on the arrival of the swallow in
the spring." Such were indeed the Greeks. How remarkable is that
Thoreau sees nothing less than *godlike*-ness in "the human intercourse
with nature"!

5.

In August, 1854, his *Walden* was published and well received. Perhaps
this might have given Thoreau some prospect of improved earning. But
let us read what he writes in the *Journal* in the following month?

(9/19/1854)
Sept. 19. Thinking this afternoon of the prospect of my writing

lectures and going abroad to read them the next winter, I realized how incomparably great the advantages of obscurity and poverty which I have enjoyed so long (and may still perhaps enjoy), I thought with what more than princely, with what poetical, leisure I had spent my years hitherto, without care or engagement, fancy free. I have given myself up to nature; I have lived so many springs and summers and autumns and winters as if I had nothing else to do but *live* them, and imbibe whatever nutriment they had for me; I have spent a couple of years, for instance, with the flowers chiefly, having none other so binding engagement as to observe when they opened. . . . Ah, how I have thriven on solitude and poverty! I cannot overstate this advantage. I do not see how I could have enjoyed it, if the public had been expecting as much of me as there is danger now that they will. If I go abroad lecturing, how shall I ever recover the lost winter?[322] [italics in text]

Notice how he describes about his life in nature: "I have lived so many springs, summers...." In a similar way, one may say correctly, Thoreau "*lived* nature," not "lived *in* nature." After the successful publication of *Walden*, Thoreau found himself much on demand for public lectures, but he continued his occasional employment as a surveyor, besides lecturing. It was during this period that he writes the following entry:

(1/4/1857)
Jan. 4. After spending four or five days surveying and drawing a plan incessantly, I especially feel the necessity of putting myself in communication with nature again, to recover my tone, to withdraw out of the wearying and unprofitable world of affairs. The things I have been doing have but a fleeting and accidental importance, however much men are immersed in them, and yield very little valuable fruit. I would fain have been wading through the woods and fields and conversing with the sane snow. I thus from time to time break off my connection with eternal truths and go with the shallow stream of human affairs, grinding at the mill of Philistines; but when my task is done, with never-failing confidence I devote myself to the infinite again. It would be sweet to deal with men more, I can imagine, but where dwell they? Not in the fields which I traverse.[323]

Perhaps the reader may find Thoreau's use of the words "eternal truths" and "the infinite" in the above passage uncharacteristically abstract or even mysterious, although one could perhaps tell what he is likely referring to—that is, nature's blessing. We have already discussed his joy of being amid the society of nature.[324] But why does he occasionally use such an abstruse language? Is he ultimately a mystic? No. I find his use of such scriptural expressions comes ultimately from his deep faith in what he calls "the gospel according to this moment."[325] Before we turn to this important topic, I cite from his *Journal* a few other instances of his use of a scriptural language:

(8/12/1851)
Though man's life is trivial and handselled nature is holy and heroic. With what infinite faith and promise and moderation begins each new day.[326]

(9/7/1851)
To watch for, describe, all the divine features which I detect in Nature.
My profession is to be always on the alert to find God in nature, to know his lurking places, to attend all the oratories, the operas in nature.[327]

(11/1/1851)
This on my way to Conantum 2:30 PM. It is a bright warm November day. I feel blessed. I love my life. I warm toward all nature."[328]

(12/14/1851)
Ah, all nature is serene and immortal.[329]

(12/27/51)
The man is blessed who every day is permitted to behold anything so pure and serene as the western sky at sunset, while revolutions vex the world.[330]

6.

Another passage from "Walking":

> Above all, we cannot afford not to live in the present. He is blessed over all mortals who loses no moment of the passing life in remembering the past. Unless our philosophy hears the cock crow in every barn-yard within our horizon, it is belated. That sound commonly reminds us that we are growing rusty and antique in our employments and habits of thought. His [the cock's] philosophy comes down to a more recent time than ours. There is something suggested by it that is a newer testament,—the gospel according to this moment. He has not fallen astern; he has got up in season, in the foremost rank of time. It is an expression of the health and soundness of Nature, a brag for all the world,—healthiness as of a spring burst forth, a new fountain of the Muses, to celebrate this last instant time. Where he lives no fugitive slave laws are passed.
> . . .
> The merit of this bird's strain is in its freedom from all plaintiveness. The singer can easily move us to tears or to laughter, but where is he who can excite in us a pure morning joy? . . . .[331]

I take the phrase "the gospel according to this moment" to mean the gospel according to *the present moment*—reading "this moment" to refer not only to this *particular* moment (namely, of the cock's crowing) but also at the same time to *any given* moment. Thus read, the "gospel" is precisely what the opening sentence of the paragraph says: "live in the present." One reads this idea of "live in the present (moment)" often expressed in *Walden* and in the *Journal*. In this passage, however, this gospel is delivered by the crowing cock at the dawn. Thoreau recognizes in the bird's crowing his "philosophy" and announces it to be our "newer testament," by which to live. Some may wonder whether one should take this particular pronouncement so seriously as to read it as an expression of Thoreau's fundamental item of faith. But read the following epigraph, which appears on the original title page of *Walden*: "I do not propose to write an ode to dejection, but to brag as lustily as chanticleer in the morning, standing on his roost, if only to wake my neighbors up."[332]

What is it to live in the present moment? It is none other than being *alive to* the present: namely, mindful seeing/mindful living. (Recall our earlier discussion of his idea of aliveness.) In this state, the mind is present where the body is, so that the mind perceives what the body perceives—one might say, the mind lives the body's life. This is exactly what Thoreau finds in the crowing chanticleer's state of being at dawn. It is in this immediate sense that he may be understood to have *lived* all those particular moments in the woods, which he records in his *Journal*.

I cite below two passages from *Walden*. In the first quotation, Thoreau calls the life in the present a *blessed* one; and in the second, he identifies the present as *God's moment*.

> We should be blessed if we lived in the present always, took advantage of every accident that befell us, like the grass which confesses the influence of the slightest dew that falls on it; and did not spend our time in atoning the neglect of past opportunities, which we call our duty. We loiter in winter while it is already spring.[333]

> Men esteem truth remote, in the outskirts of the system, behind the farthest star, before Adam and after the last man. In eternity there is indeed something true and sublime. But all these times and places and occasions are now and here. God himself culminates in the present moment, and will never be more divine in the lapse of all the ages[334]

In this second passage, we see once again Thoreau's scriptural language. Here, however, he sounds much like Kierkegaard, as he claims that "truth" is not something you find outside "all these times and places and occasions: it is to be found here and now." Isn't he here speaking of "eternal present"? Let us keep in mind that the kind of "truth" he is speaking of is not that of an abstract idea or proposition, but of living experience.

In one diary entry (6/22/1851), Thoreau asks himself: what is "the kind of life to which I am thus continually allured? which alone I love?" He then goes on questioning further:

> Is it a life for this world? Can a man feed and clothe himself gloriously who keeps only the truth steadily before him? who calls in no evil to his aid? Are there duties which necessarily interfere with the serene perception of truth? Are our serene moments mere foretastes of heaven,—joys gratuitously vouchsafed to us as a

consolation,—or simply a transient realization of what might be the whole tenor of our lives?[335]

A man "who keeps only the truth steadily before him" must be one who "lives in the present." Let us take seriously Thoreau's phrase "the serene perception of truth." The "truth" serenely perceived must be a truth that one discovers only in a meditative awareness, namely in mindfulness. He is here speaking clearly of the sort of truth that would give life deeper meaning.

Earlier, we saw Thoreau write in his *Journal*: "I thus from time to time break off my connection with eternal truths and go with the shallow stream of human affairs, grinding at the mill of Philistines; but when my task is done, with never failing confidence I devote myself to the infinite again." By "eternal truths," he does not mean any truth metaphysical or mysterious; for him they are nowhere outside nature—that is, outside the present. Let us recall his statement: "My profession is to be always on the alert to find God in nature." In his serene, mindful moment, Thoreau sees nature divine and infinite.

7.

In early December of 1860, Thoreau caught a severe cold, which resulted in bronchitis and kept him housebound all winter. His underlying health problem was tuberculosis. In the summer of 1861, Thoreau traveled to Minnesota in his attempt to improve his deteriorating condition, but returned to Concord early July in worse condition than when he set out. He never recovers his health and dies in the following May, at the age of forty-four. No entry in the *Journal* after his return mentions his walking in the woods. But one still reads some remarks that indicate his undiminished interest as a naturalist. In one place, he even notes "a large hornets' nest on a maple (September 29), the *half-immersed* leaves turned scarlet."[336] Interestingly, though, he reports in the penultimate entry of the *Journal*, his close observation of the growing weeks of four newly-born kittens. The following are excerpts from his progress report on the kittens:

Four little kittens just born; lay like stuffed skins of kittens in a heap, with pink feet; so flimsy and helpless they lie, yet blind, without any stiffness or ability to stand.

. . . .

The kitten can already spit at a fortnight old, and it can mew from the first, though it often makes the motion of mewing without uttering any sound.

. . . .

The kittens' ears are at first neatly concealed in the fur, and at a fortnight old they are mere broad-based triangles with a side foremost. . . .

At three weeks old the kitten begins to walk in a staggering and creeping manner and even to play a little with its mother, and, if you put your ear close, you may hear it purr. . . .

I saw it scratch its ear to-day, probably for the first time; yet it lifted one of its hind legs and scratched its ear as effectually as an old cat does. . . .[337]

Is it strange that these new lives' coming into being should have attracted this dying man's interest more than anything else? After all, Thoreau was "always on the alert to find God" in the present.

Notes to the Appendices

286 The original title of Tao's *gui qulai xi ci* has the character *ci* at the end, which has commonly referred to a certain distinct form of literature since the Han times. In this special sense, it is often called also *fu*. Arthur Waley regards *fu* as "descriptive prose-poems,, unrhymed but more or less metrical." (See A. Waley, trans., *A Hundred and Seventy Chinese Poems* (London: Constable & Co., 1918), p. 13.) From a standpoint of versification, James J. Y. Liu goes one step further to assert that *fu* may better be regarded as a "literary genre" rather than as a "verse form." (See James J. Y. Liu, *The Art of Chinese Poetry* (Chicago: The University of Chicago Press, 1962), pp. 33–4.) I am inclined to go along with Waley's idea of *fu* here. In any case, the style of *gui qulai xi ci* more than justifies our calling it a poem in its broad sense—that is, in the sense in which the Chinese people today use the character *shi*.

287 On <www.silkqin.com>. These lines are followed by "Original preface," "Music and lyrics: One Section," and "Footnotes."

288 We are here considering only the first three characters, since they alone determine the meaning of the phrase, since the character "*xi*" is merely a poetic particle without any special meaning of its own, and *ci* simply means this particular form of poem.

289 Matsueda Shigeo and Wada Takeshi, *Toenmei Zensh* (The Complete Work of Tao Yuanming"), 2 vols. (Tokyo: Iwanami Shoten, 2010). See their note on the title of this poem in Vol. 2, pp. 138–9. I am entirely indebted to these two co-authors for clarification of the meaning of the title.

290 *Op. cit.,* p. 138. In the same note, they also cite the following line from a song written in Chinese by a Japanese poet, included in *Many sh* : "*qulai zideng zao riben bian*" ("Let us all quickly return to Japan"). *Many sh* is a collection of poems, compiled in 759, which presumably included many poems written in Chinese in earlier ages.

291. I have checked over the internet how the Japanese and the Koreans have taken the phrase in question to mean. Their common translations indicate that they too, traditionally, seem to have read "*gui qu-lai*" in the sense of "let [us/me] return"—i.e., as a phrase of urging.

292 Yip, *Chinese Poetry*, p. 23.

293 Witter Bynner, *The Jade Mountain* (New York, 1919), p. 119. Cited in Yip, *Chinese Poetry*, p. 23.

294 Yip, *Chinese Poetry*, p. 23.

295 A few words about what is known as *prose poem*. Is this term an oxymoron? Of course not. Yes, in terms of form, a prose poem is a piece of prose. To read it as a poem, however, one must move from image to image, which is in fact to read it poetically, not conceptually. In this sense, prose poems are poems which happen to take the form of prose.

296 I have previously introduced the difference between the thinking mind and the seeing mind in my works, *To See God, To See the Buddha* (Brighton: Sussex Academic Press, 2010) and *Beyond Words, Things, Thoughts, Feelings* (Brighton: Sussex Academic Press, 2011).

297 *The Poetics of Space*, trans. Maria Jolas (Boston: Beacon Press, 1994), p. xv.

298 *The Days of Henry Thoreau* (New York: Alfred A. Knopf, 1965), p. ix.

299 *Walden and Other Writing of Henry David Thoreau*, ed. Brooks Atkinson (New York: The Modern Library, 1992), p. 645. All references to "Walking" are to this Modern Library edition.

300 *Walden and Other Writing of Henry David Thoreau*, ed. Brooks Atkinson (New York: The Modern Library, 1992), p. 105. All references to *Walden* are to this Modern Library edition. Italics added.

301 *The Journal of Henry D. Thoreau* (1837–October 1855), eds. Bradford Torrey and Francis H. Allen (New York: Dover Publications, 1962), p. 204. Italics added. This edition is hereafter abbreviated simply as "*Journal*."

302 "Walking," p. 632. Italics added.

303 *Walden*, pp. 105–7. Italics added.

304 *The Journal 1837–1861: Henry David Thoreau*, ed. Damion Searls (New

York: New York Review Books, 2009), p. 34. This edition of the *Journal* is hereafter abbreviated as "*Journal* (37–61)."

305 *Journal* (37–61), p. 41.
306 *Journal*, p. 167.
307 *Journal*, p. 196.
308 Ibid.
309 *Journal* (37–61), p. 453.
310 *Journal* (37–61), p. 342.
311 *Journal*, p. 441.
312 *Journal*, p. 185.
313 *Journal*, p. 226.
314 *Journal*, p. 275.
315 "Walking," p. 652.
316 *Journal*, p. 299.
317 Ibid.
318 Clearly indicative of his rejection of the Cartesian dualism of mind and body.
319 Walden, p. 123.
320 "Walking," pp. 650–51.
321 Robert Sattelmeyer, ed. *Henry D. Thoreau: Journal*, Vol. 2. Princeton: Princeton University Press, 1984), pp. 233–234.
322 *Journal*, p. 806.
323 *Journal* (37–61), p. 429.
324 Or, rather, "society in nature," as Thoreau once uses this phrase in his *Journal* (April 18, 1846) during his stay in Walden Pond. He writes:
I have never felt lonely or in the least oppressed by a sense of solitude but once, and that was a few weeks after I came here to live when for an hour I doubted if the near neighborhood of man was not essential to a healthy life. To be alone was something. But I was at the same time conscious of a slight insanity —and seemed to foresee my recovery—in the midst of a gentle rain while these thoughts prevailed— [sic] There suddenly seemed such sweet and beneficent society in nature—and the very pattering of the drops—& in every sound and sight around my house—as made fancied advantages of human neighborhood insignificant. I was so distinctly made aware of the presence of my *kindred*, even in scenes which are accustomed to call wild, that the nearest blood to me & humanist was not a person nor a villager—that no place could be strange to me.
Cheerful society is worthy employment. (Italics in text) (See Robert Sattelmeyer, ed. *Henry D. Thoreau: Journal*, Vol. 2. Princeton: Princeton University Press, 1984, pp. 235–236.)
325 "Walking," p. 662.

326 *Journal*, p. 240.

327 *Journal*, p. 262.

328 *Journal*, p. 296.

329 *Journal*, p. 309.

330 *Journal*, p. 314.

331 "Walking," p. 662. Italics added.

332 This sentence also appears in the text of *Walden* ("Where I Lived, and What I Lived For"), p. 80.

333 *Walden*, p. 295. See also *Walden*, pp. 16, 105, and "Walking," p. 662.

334 *Walden*, p. 92.

335 *Journal*, p. 211.

336 *Journal* (37–61), p. 665.

337 *Journal* (37–61), pp. 665–6.

Bibliography

1. Primary Sources
(The following works contain the original Chinese texts together with Japanese translations and notes.)

Part One

(1) Fujino Iwatomo, trans. *Soji (Chu Ci)*. Tokyo: Shūeisha, 1996.
(2) Matsueda Shigeo, trans. *Chūkoku shisen*, (An Anthology of Chinese Poems), Vol. 1. Tokyo: Iwanami Shoten, 1992.
(3) Mekada Makoto, trans. *Shikyō Soji (Shi Jing* and *Chu Ci)*. Tokyo: Heibonsha, 1979.
(4) Shirakawa Shizuka, trans. *Shikyō Kokufū (Shi Jing Guo Feng)*. Tokyo: Heibonsha, 1990.
(5) Takata Shinji, trans. *Shikyō (Shi Jing)*, 2 volumes. Tokyo: Sh eisha, 1996..

Part Two

(1) Ikkai Tomoyoshi, ed. *Riku Yū Shisen* (Poems of Lu Yu). Tokyo: Iwanami Shoten, 2007.
(2) Kawai Kōzō, trans. *Hakurakuten Shisen* (Poems of Bai Keyi), 2 vols. Tokyo: Iwanami Shoten, 2011.
(3) Kurokawa Yōichi, ed. *To Ho Shisen* (Poems of Du Fu). Tokyo: Iwanami Shoten, 2011.
(4) Maeno Naoaki, trans. *Tōshisen (Tang Shi Xuan* [An Anthology of Poems of Tang]), 3 vols. Tokyo: Iwanami Shoten, 2011.
(5) Matsueda Shigeo, trans. *Chūkoku Meishisen*, (An Anthology of Chinese Poems), 3 vols. Tokyo: Iwanami Shoten, 1992, 93, 92.
(6) Matsueda Shigeo, Wada Takeshi, trans. *Tōenmei Zenshū* (The Complete Works of Tao Yuanming), 2 vols. Tokyo: Iwanami Shoten, 2010.
(7) Matsuura Tomohisa, trans. *Ri Haku Shishū* (Poems of Li Bai). Tokyo: Iwanami Shoten, 2012.
(8) Ogawa Tamaki, Tsuru Haruo, Iritani Sensuke, trans. *Ō I Shishū* (Poems of Wang Wei) . Tokyo: Iwanami Shoten, 1990.
(9) Ogawa Tamaki, Yamamoto Kazuyoshi, trans. *So Tōha Shisen* (Poems of Su Shi). Tokyo: Iwanami Shoten, 2011.

(10) Shimosada Masahiro, trans. *Ryū Sōgen Sshisen* (Poems of Liu Zongyuan). Tokyo: Iwanami Shoten, 2011.

2. Other References

(Listed below are English publications referred to in the book, except in Appendix 3.)

Bynner, Witter, trans. *The Jade Mountain.* New York, 1919.

Graham, A. C. trans. *Poems of The Late T'ang.* New York: New York Review of Books, 1965.

Hawkes, David, trans. *The Songs of the South: An Ancient Chinese Anthology of Poems by Qu Yuan and Other Poets.* London: Penguin Books, 1985.

Jolas Maria, trans. *The Poetics of Space* (*La poétique de l'espace* by Gaston Bachelard). Boston: Beacon Press, 1994.

Liu, James J. Y. *The Art of Chinese Poetry.* Chicago: The University of Chicago Press, 1962.

Waley, Arthur, trans. *A Hundred and Seventy Chinese Poems.* London: Constable & Co., 1918.

_____, trans. *The Book of Songs.* New York: Grove Press, 1937.

Yip, Wai-lim, trans. *Chinese Poetry.* Berkeley: University of California Press, 1976.

_____. *Ezra Pound's Cathay.* Princeton: Princeton University Press, 1969.

3. References in Appendix 3

Atkinson, Brooks, ed. *Walden and Other Writings of Henry David Thoreau.* New York: The Modern Library, 1992.

Harding, Walter. *The Days of Henry Thoreau.* New York: Alfred A. Knopf. 1965.

Sattelmeyer, Robert, ed. *Henry D. Thoreau: Journal*, Vol. 2. Princeton: Princeton University Press, 1984.

Searls, Damien, ed. *The Journal of 1837–1861: Henry David Thoreau.* New York: New York Review Books, 2009.

Torrey, Bradford and Francis H. Allen, eds. *The Journal of Henry D. Thoreau (1837–1855).* New York: Dover Publications, 1962.

Printed and bound by CPI Group (UK) Ltd, Croydon, CR0 4YY

09/06/2025

14685943-0001